Pass It On

Interviews by Youth with Mentors That Matter

BY THE STUDENTS OF WHAT KIDS CAN DO, INC.

Edited by Kathleen Cushman

NEXT GENERATION PRESS
Providence, Rhode Island

Printed in Hong Kong by South Sea International Press Ltd.
Distributed by Next Generation Press, Providence, Rhode Island

ISBN 0-9762706-8-4
CIP data available.

Book design by Sandra Delany.

Cover photograph by Jennie Carson, of Ricardo Pitts-Wiley, artistic director
of Mixed Magic Theatre, with Rudy Cabrera, Central High School student,
in Providence, RI.

Photograph on page viii by Will Okun, of Ada Kadishson Schieber with
student at the Chicago mentors celebratory event.

Next Generation Press, a not-for-profit book publisher, brings forward the voices
and vision of adolescents on their own lives, learning, and work. With a particular
focus on youth without economic privilege, Next Generation Press raises awareness
of young people as a powerful force for social justice.

Next Generation Press, P.O. Box 603252, Providence, RI 02906
www.nextgenerationpress.org

10 9 8 7 6 5 4 3 2 1

Contents

Preface

REGULAR INTERACTION WITH CARING ADULTS is vital to young people's development. Of the factors that influence students to do well in school and take on productive roles in the community, the supportive relationships they form in their adolescent years are extremely important.

Parents and teachers have enormous influence in the lives of young people. In the high school years, however, teenagers begin looking beyond home and school for new connections, ideas, fellow feeling, and inspiration. In fact, they often intentionally turn to someone who is not their parent or teacher – who can see them in new ways, without the defining, familiar frame that home or school may unwittingly impose.

In the Mentors That Matter project, high school students from four cities nominated for recognition ordinary adults – outside their homes and classrooms – who guide, inspire and help develop their strengths. The students then interviewed and photographed their mentors, who come from all walks of life. Some are well known in their communities; others are known only to the people whose lives they directly touch.

In this book, we hear first-person accounts from a school bus driver, hair stylist, and many other ordinary people who give of themselves to other people's children, even when it is not their job to do so. Although they come from Chicago, Providence, San Francisco, and Tampa, their stories echo those of thousands of adults all over the country, who have found satisfaction, if not public recognition in the same way.

As the students documented what the adults told them, other important benefits emerged from the project. Students began to practice the skills of professional journalists: framing good questions, interviewing, taking strong photographs, transcribing, editing, and shaping their material into essay form. As they initiated discussions with their nominees, the young people also gained visibly in courage, self-respect, and faith in their own potential. In each city, at a culminating Mentors That Matter event, students hung gleaming medals around the necks of the adults they had chosen to honor. Mutual pride and pleasure showed on the faces of both youth and mentors.

MetLife Foundation supported this project to draw

national attention to the value and significance of the mentoring relationship for both youth and adults. When someone reaches out to a youth, he or she strengthens the social fabric of our communities, with consequences far beyond the moment. We hope that readers of this book will themselves feel moved to connect with a young person. We are all teachers, this book reminds us, and we have much to learn about, and from, each other.

Sibyl Jacobson
President, MetLife Foundation
September 2007

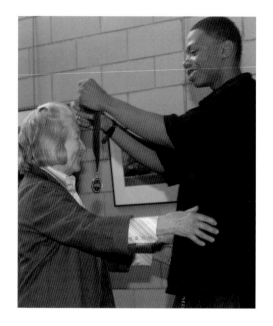

Pass It On

*Whatever you learned, you have to pass it on
to the younger generation.*

Susheela Nathan, pediatrician

Stories Are Breathing

Len Cabral, Storyteller
INTERVIEW BY Marcus Page and Jason Page
Central High School, Providence

ORKING AT A DAY CARE CENTER in South Providence, I discovered storytelling as a teaching tool. I would ask children questions: "You ride a bike, what color is your bike? Where do you bike? You had an accident, and you had stitches – tell me that story." After that, they got to tell their own story again, but this time I would not ask the questions. I want people to realize: You have stories, you have the voice. If you do not tell your story, someone else will. You know your story better, and you can tell it best.

When I was growing up, my parents were separated, but there were positive male role models around that helped me to get through rough spots in my life. I realized how important it was for young children to have male teachers. There are enough men out there with basketballs, hockey sticks, with weapons. But we do not see men promoting nurturing things: reading, education.

I think we all need more mentors. I could find trouble as a kid, but I had to go look for it. But for you kids, trouble comes knocking at the door, trouble comes on the computer, trouble comes over the phone. So I try to find stories that help people deal with their lives, the rough spots that face students today. There are some wonderful tales from Africa dealing with strength. People confuse strength with being a bully. A bully has a crack in his character, and a crack is a weakness, not strength. Real strength is about the inner self.

I encourage young people to interview their parents and grandparents and listen to their stories. When we connect to the elders in the community, we can get wisdom. There is an African saying, "When elders die, it is like a library burning." No matter what culture you are from, your ancestors told stories. So when we tell stories about our weekend, we are doing something that people have been doing ever since the beginning of time. People have always eaten and they have always told stories. That connects us to our history.

I have been telling stories for thirty years. I do not care how old the listeners are, you can feel and see how they, too, experience the story. You are not passively listening, you are actively participating, you are using your imagination. You have to visualize the characters, the movement – and on top of that, the empathy that you may have for the character, the wondering, the trance that we go into as we listen. It's a lot of work for the mind. You sit listening to a story, you get tired!

That is why stories are so important, as opposed to sitting and watching television or music videos. All that stuff has stimulation. Stories are breathing. You are affecting the stories. Feel that! Think that!

Pass It On

Edith Lewis, police officer
INTERVIEW BY Brittany Tucker
Leadership High School, San Francisco

I GREW UP IN CHICAGO, ON THE SOUTH SIDE, and also in San Francisco – the Western Addition, the Alemany housing projects, and the Potrero Hill housing projects. I went to school at Woodrow Wilson High, with predominantly African-Americans, Latinos, and Samoans. I was a pretty good student, very involved in sports and school activities. I had a job after school at the Park and Rec facility. It was a community, family, village type environment. Someone helped me, so I knew I had to pass it on.

When I was living in the housing projects, I always took time out to play with the younger kids, taking them to the park, the movies, the store, telling stories, playing games. It just carried over when I became a cop. I've been working with kids throughout the whole city for the last eighteen-plus years, saving as many as I possibly can. I work with babies all the way up to eighteen, nineteen years old.

Sometimes kids put up barriers. They don't want to give you the chance to know them, because they're hurting for whatever reason. Maybe they don't trust me as an officer, or as an adult, or as a female. They think that we were not kids at one time. They wanna do things their own way, without any help.

That's my passion – to try to reach them, to teach them, to help them believe in themselves. I just like being in the presence of young people, it doesn't matter what age or nationality, or what group people want to categorize them in. I like seeing that they're doing well, that they're trying to better themselves.

I can be driving down the street and people be yelling, "Hey, Officer Lewis, remember this or that?" Kids thank me. They're like, "You were the only one that really cared." I tell them that I wasn't doing my job to be mean, but to make them understand: I had a job and they had a job, and my job was to make sure that they went to school and to class.

When you help a kid, at the end of the day, hopefully they'll be able to pass it on. Maybe you take time just talking to them, sharing a story, listening to them, crying with them, or just taking them somewhere where they can talk to you, one on one. Whatever I give them, I tell them to pass it on to the next generation.

Been Knowing Them for a Long Time

Georgia Dunbar, school bus driver
INTERVIEW BY Kendra Clark
and Brittney Williams
ACT Charter School, Chicago

I AM A SCHOOL BUS DRIVER. I'm pretty much gone fourteen hours a day, driving from six in the morning to six in the evening. I sometimes spend more time with the teenagers on my bus than I do with my own daughter. I pick them up and take them to school. We talk, they tell me about things going on at home in their lives, their friends. And then I take them back home.

I started driving the school bus in 2002. I was tired of being a nurse assistant and, I was just looking through the paper one day and I seen an ad for school bus drivers. I really like the kids, so I guess that's why I've been doing it for so long. I'm probably like their second mom, I guess I can say, because I've been knowing them for a long time and taking them back and forth to school. I kind of look out for them and make sure they get to school safe and get home safe.

When I was a teenager I spent a lot of time with my aunt, and with my family and friends. When you hang around older people, they show you a lot of things and teach you a lot of things. I learned how to be independent, work hard, and take care of family, because family means everything. I'm there for my family all the time, if they need me to do things for them, like take my grandmother back and forth to the doctor.

Teens are very smart, and they act like they know everything. I guess they are more independent then we were when we were younger. They have more freedom than we had, and they have a lot more stuff, like cell phones and credit cards. It was not like this when we were growing up. We pretty much had to rely on our parents. This generation, they really pretty much handle themselves. But I try to tell them they don't know everything.

Being around the young kids makes me feel younger and keeps me more alive and wanting to go to work. My job is very easy, but it also can get difficult if the kids is not nice. The kids being very nice and respectable, that makes me motivated to keep going. Some of my kids that move on and go away, we still talk. Sometimes we'll get together, maybe go out to the movies or just sit around and talk.

I tell kids: Just stay in school. Whatever goal you want to accomplish in life, just don't let nobody tell you that you can't do it. Just keep striving. Keep going on.

Saying Nothing

Brother Damian McCullagh,
elder at Tampa Catholic, copy machine guru
INTERVIEW BY Ryan Carter and Taylor Neal
Mayor's Youth Corps, Tampa

I N HIGH SCHOOL, I WAS A TYPICAL, bashful, quiet sophomore. I loved the school I was at. It was the first time ever I met Christian Brothers. I was terrified of them, because they were so strict. I met this brother who used to play the piano. Five or six of us used to gather around the piano and we would play what you would call today rock and roll. I was surprised he knew all these things. I thought brothers went to this place to pray all by themselves, and the world was left behind.

That brother says, "Did you ever think of becoming a Christian Brother?" I was so embarrassed I couldn't say anything.

A month goes by. He says, "Martin McCullagh, what did you come to?" I said, "They would never take me. They'll hate me. I think I'm not good enough to be a brother." He says, "You don't have to be good enough. You want to be good enough, that's why you join."

I was a full time teacher for 52 years. I started in grammar school and high school. Then I worked at a college in admissions. I used to go around and get young girls and young guys to go to college there. I loved it. You meet the nicest people in the world.

Now that I'm retired, I have to do something. I'm in charge of all the copying at the high school. It occupies me for several hours a day. I call it the cave, where I work – no windows.

I love talking to the guys, and they like talking to me. I have set things that I say: "How about that smile?" Or a guy goes by, and I say, "Smile, because you only have one more class to go." Simple things like this. I used to put that down, as something not consequential or important.

One day, I was like, "You can smile now. You got a free day. You got a long weekend." And the boy looked at me and he started to cry. Uh-oh, I said the wrong thing. I didn't know. He told me everything. He was fighting at home with his parents. And they pretty well told him, "You're a good-for-nothing. I'm sorry we ever brought you into this world." That's like being cut in two by family. His marks went down awfully fast. He felt useless. I don't know if what I said meant anything.

Later, I realized he doesn't want me to say anything. He just wants me to listen.

When I started, I had to be the speaker. I had to tell the guy what to do. He would be there listening, and I would do all the talking. It should have been reversed.

Saying nothing is the best sign of mentoring. After all my mistakes, I just listened.

You can pass on only those things you experience yourself. It's like they say in writing. "Don't write anything unless you know it." How to handle the highs and lows in life, that's the hard part. A mature person comes to understand that it's not going to be easy. Students pale when I tell them: "No, you never failed. Just try again."

After fourteen years I know every corner of this restaurant like the palm of my hand, and sometimes I wonder why I am still here. Thank God, I haven't got injured; I have no benefits. But in these years of working and saving, I have been able to bring my family here, buy two houses and two cars, and, best of all, have another daughter, who made my whole life complete. All my sacrifices have been worth it, because now I have a beautiful life. My only wish is that my kids graduate and become someone important in this country, and that they work in a office – not like me.

Getting in the Ropes

Natasha Johnson, double-dutch coach
INTERVIEW BY Stephanie Carew
The Met Center, Providence

I WAS ABOUT TWELVE YEARS OLD when I first tried double-dutch, in Barbados. I taught myself, outside with the girls. When I was 28, a friend in Providence re-introduced it to me. I loved it. Our team started training for competitions. From then on, I just ran with it.

Three years ago, I started out with my own double-dutch team. It's a passion – I love my kids, man! I paid to get the team started, out of pocket. Now it's growing, it's doing good, and we have sponsors and do fundraisers. I work with kids ages eight to nineteen. Their age doesn't really matter – either you got it or you don't.

If you make it hard, then it will be hard. Practice makes perfect. You have to get in and out the ropes, and you compete in speed, compulsory, and freestyle. The easiest thing is getting in and out the ropes. For speed, you jump for two minutes without stopping, at a consistent speed. Compulsory consists of jumping eight turns clockwise, eight counter-clockwise, two crisscrosses, and ten high steps. Freestyle is really hard – you dance, do flips, and do acrobatics in the ropes. You really have to practice on that to get good.

You can tell a lot about a kid from how they jump rope. When they do a trick they could never do, their self-esteem just rises. I had one student who was having problems at home. I told her she could do the tricks – she just had to keep her mind off her problems. Now she is one of my best jumpers. She still has problems at home, but when she gets in the ropes, she forgets about them.

The kids learn to respect themselves and others, and to just "be you." In this business, everybody has a different personality. I don't call it bad, it's just their personality. When they do something they are not supposed to do, I give them pushups.

It's important to me to be a mentor to these kids. If I had a mentor, back when I was that age, maybe someone would have pushed me into accomplishing all my goals sooner. I rearranged my class schedule in college, to dedicate at least two days a week for them.

Everywhere the kids go, everybody wants to see them perform. We do a lot, and we're going to do so much more.

Hard Cover

Tom Bailey, television producer
INTERVIEW BY Bridgett Rivers
ACT Charter School, Chicago

I WORK WITH YOUTH at Community TV Network, where I started a TV program called Hard Cover. The youth that come to the after-school program are entirely responsible for producing all the shows that go on Hard Cover. I am involved in training the youth and then helping them with the production of the show. I work with about 35 to 40 students now, and over the past two and a half years I've worked with probably five or six hundred.

I thought I was going to be doing a lot of acting and doing films and theater at the same time. But most of my energy is focused on working with youth. I'm only able to do my creative work maybe 20 hours a week, instead of 40 to 60 hours a week.

The interactions that I have with my students are more informal than at school, where it is teacher and student and a much more defined relationship. I feel more like a big brother figure and less like a teacher or a parent. It's more like co-workers, working together to produce the show.

Sometimes the motivation just isn't there to learn and progress and succeed. I try to relate what I teach to the everyday lives of youth. If they understood how a principle relates to them in everyday life, they might be more interested in learning. The most important thing is to be an independent thinker. To think for yourself and not just take ideas from what the others are saying. To find your own truth that means something to you.

Structure is something that I've tried to use in every program that I run. It is very specific, and within that structure there are areas for creativity and areas to do what youth want. I am surprised how quickly the young people I work with adapt to change. When I introduce a new concept, or something changes, there seems to be some resistance at first. But they are fast learners and they pick up things very quickly, especially with respect to technology.

I've had the opportunity to travel with some students and to win a few awards along the way for the work youth have done here. When they are recognized for it, I do feel a sense of accomplishment. Those are moments that they'll perhaps remember for the rest of their lives.

I learn stuff most every day, and that's a great thing. When youth bring a new idea to the table, something I haven't thought of before, it's a really great feeling for me. That's a great side benefit of the job. They often inspire me to put some of these ideas into my own ideas.

Mentorship 101

James Geiger, counselor, Anytown program
INTERVIEW BY Simon and Manuela Muñoz-Alvarez
and Alexa Holcomb
Mayor's Youth Corps, Tampa

I WAS BORN NINE WEEKS EARLY, one pound two ounces. I was the size of a dollar bill. And on top of all that, I was born dead. I had no heartbeat, so I didn't have oxygen to my brain, causing parts of my brain cells to die off. The doctors predicted I would never walk or talk.

My childhood was difficult. My family was a military family, so I moved every two to three years. I never had any lifelong friends like most kids. I thought that I would be a person who people pick on, day in and day out.

I participated in Anytown as a delegate once, in ninth grade. It's a national program, a week-long diversity and leadership training for high school students from fourteen to eighteen. I asked the director if I could go home, because I was not enjoying myself. I wanted to be with my mom and dad. He said, "You have to stick it out." He would not let me go home. That stuck with me my whole life. If I would have gone home, I wouldn't be the person I am today.

I've just finished my eighth Anytown as a counselor. On the first day, when the delegates come on the big bus, I get a pump of adrenaline. Who's going to be on that bus? Who's going to be closed-minded and not want to talk to me? But by the very last day we are best friends. And of course, on the last day I am very sad. Because we have built this community, but then after Anytown they go their separate ways.

I didn't think that I could be a mentor, because I was disabled. No one would want me to help out. I never imagined I could have this much impact. I was elected to the Advisory Board, which plans Anytown for next year. I have subcommittees which I check upon each month and I guide them so that we can make sure that this summer goes out with a hit. I'm creating a documentary about Anytown with a couple of student filmmakers.

I am not getting paid for any of this. This is because I love the program so freaking much. I think mentoring has always been in my personality. I never took a class like mentorship 101. It is in my nature: I love to help and I love people. No matter how old I am, no matter what I'm into, I want to keep that line of communication open.

You are going to come across people who look or talk different than you, who may have a different lifestyle or funky hair, whatever it may be. You have to keep an open mind. We are all human. Genetically, we are 99.99 percent alike. If you degrade the person you sit next to, you are basically degrading a brother or sister. If you make any limits, you can limit the stuff you are going to learn.

Fragile but Dangerous

Naomi Wright, assistant, after-school program
INTERVIEW BY Prisca Cheng
Leadership High School, San Francisco

WHEN I WAS A KID it was a whole different world from what you see now. Now people put low expectations on youths. More people tell them, "You can't do it." Everybody can grow. If it's someone who's getting an F, he can raise it to a D. They can change and learn how to deal with their anger and frustration. They just lack self-esteem and a goal.

I used to teach youths in the city about the ecology of the Muir Woods. A lot of them didn't have cars, and most of them had never left the city. It was just great, showing them a whole different world that is only about thirty minutes away. From that, I just realized that I want to work with youth.

Now I am in charge of the day-to day-operations of the after-school program in James Denman Middle School. I live in the Sunset, and it's weird: You go to different neighborhoods where they put a lot more money and investment in the schools. There's no lights by our basketball courts, so the kids can't play after dark. Environment matters; it shows the investment they have in youth. I don't know if they just have more faith in the youths in other neighborhoods. In San Francisco, they track you from middle school and on to the opportunities you will have in life. I don't feel it's fair.

I don't see a lot of adults stepping up even though they are not parents. Every adult should be helping a child, helping them grow as people. In some way, it is your responsibility. I don't have kids, but this is just how I feel.

Working here gave me an appreciation for how difficult it is to be a parent as well as how difficult it is to be a kid. When I was a girl, to gain power and be important in the world, your goals were to become a doctor or a lawyer. It seems like young girls now try to get attention or power through dressing. It doesn't seem like there is a lot of positive influences in youth life today.

I love middle school and high school, because they are able to look at things in different ways. They're learning who they are as people. They're fragile and dangerous at the same time, like firecrackers. You set them off, and once you do it is really really beautiful. Everybody can see them shine.

Cooking Teaches You to Think Ahead

Steve Bianchini, restaurant chef
INTERVIEW BY Cheyla Luciano
and Janaye Ramos
The Met Center, Providence

I HATED SCHOOL. I did pretty good in it, I just didn't like it. It didn't keep my interest. I was kind of like the ringleader. But I was good at cooking. Some people have a gift, that's my gift.

I was poor when I was a kid. I started working when I was thirteen, washing dishes and scrubbing floors and washing out pots and pans. You work at that job for a couple years, then you get a promotion to flipping hamburgers and cooking French fries. After that I just picked it up, and I started working at my uncle's and father's restaurant, too. I got a lot of training there. I learned the hard way and became successful by working extra hard.

I ended up working right away after high school, for different operations, like Pawtucket Country Club. When I was eighteen, I moved to New Hampshire, right near the mountains. I worked for the Marriott for thirteen years in the food and beverage department, opening up hotels throughout the country. My uncle and father taught me how to save money, and to invest the money I earned. Now I have two restaurants [Meritage in East Greenwich, Rhode Island, and Chardonnay's in Seekonk, Massachusetts].

Managing restaurants is very difficult, 'cause you're working with people every day of the week. Conducting business the proper way means being a good person, not trying to get over on people. If someone works for you, you pay them. And you treat them with respect.

Cooking teaches you how to plan out things, to think ahead. You have an idea and place it into play, and create a great dish that people would like. You have to know math to extend recipes. You also have to research the products that you're going to buy for certain dishes – you have to able to get the product, and it has to be cost effective. And you have to know how to prepare the raw product. You have to have great taste buds, so the dish is good. Then you have to teach the dish to the cooks that work for you, and check the dish periodically, so it remains as good as you created it. When you cook you have to please people – it's a lot easier in life if you are in harmony. So you also have to compromise when cooking.

You get to a point in life when it's not about the money, it's about giving back to the community. If I can help someone that is young and trying to improve themselves, maybe I can make a difference in someone's life. I would be happy if someone said, "I remember going to Steve's restaurant, and I'm a chef now because of him."

I See Leadership in You

Dwayne Sanders, student government adviser
INTERVIEW BY Shakira Robinson,
Christopher Smith, and Vivian Taylor
ACT Charter School, Chicago

WHEN I WAS IN HIGH SCHOOL, I didn't want to spend any time with any adults. I didn't want anything to do with school or teachers. I had other plans for myself: I was going to be a defense attorney or a really good prosecutor. But one of my teachers told me, "I see leadership in you and you should take advantage of that." I was one of the few black students at a mostly white school. I can name the black kids at my school on four fingers, and that's not counting me. For that teacher to just come up to me and say "I see that in you" was special. From there I ended up running for student council and becoming its vice president and then president.

I think that everybody has something that they are destined to do, and when you find it you feel comfortable. Seven years ago I just fell into teaching when I was working for the Chicago Department of Health. One of the founders of this school wanted me to come here and teach video.

Right now, my main job is to deal with students who can't behave or control themselves in class. As an adviser or mentor, you just have to figure out which solution would fit that kid – not which one is easier

for you. Sometimes you have to beat the kid over the head with a stick and sometimes you have to take a step back and watch them fail. Sometimes it means listening and coming up with a solution with them. We underestimate teens sometimes. They can do more than what we give them credit for.

The kids who are part of student government, some of them struggle after high school, but they always have some skill they've learned to fall back on. When I see students plan stuff for other things, and I know they've learned how to do this through student government, I appreciate that. My inspiration is the moments that I see the kids that have succeeded and are proud of something.

The Brain Is the Most Wonderful Organ

Susheela Nathan, pediatrician,
and *Ravindra Nathan*, cardiologist[*]
INTERVIEW BY Shreya Narayanan
and Alena Ransom
Mayor's Youth Corps, Tampa

URING SUMMER VACATION WHEN I was in med school, some of the neighborhood children and teens wanted to ask me questions, clear their doubts, and get help with their homework. Because many of their essays were science or math, their parents would encourage them: "Oh, Ravi is back here from school, so why don't you go ask him." Back at home in Kerala, people will drop into your house and visit with you. When they ask you for your help, you don't feel like saying no, especially when it is something close to your heart.

After I became a pediatrician, I used to sit down and chat with my patients and help them sort out their problems, especially with school. You see so many people wasting their potential, because they don't have the proper guidance. If you have an interest in arts, or sports, you should develop that. But I always told youngsters, "Your priority should be developing your brain, which is the most wonderful organ."

We have been involved with middle school and high school children of this area for many years, directing science fair projects. In fact, we were the Institutional Review Board for every medical project which students conducted during those years. And both of us were judges for the Florida Junior Academy of Sciences. We were very much into science teaching and coaching.

I would tell my patients that they should enter with a science project. They would ask for ideas and I would mention something simple that they could start with. Then they would bring their projects and abstracts for correction. I used to guide them through that.

I am a scientist, and I tell students: If you become a good scientist, it doesn't matter if it's mathematics, computers, medicine, engineering. Whatever it is, there is going to be a job for you. We cannot live without science.

Whatever you learn in your childhood usually stays with you. Some children don't mind being forced, but many children don't like it. However, there is a fine line between guiding and forcing. If you have no interest, you will not succeed. It depends on your level of interest, and how much you can put into it. Basically that's the equation.

Whatever you learned, you have to pass it on to the younger generation.

---

[*] Dr. Susheela Nathan's words appear in italics, Dr. Ravindra Nathan's words in roman type.

I'm Right Where I Want to Be

Andres Fernandez, capoeira teacher
INTERVIEW BY Edwin Lara
Leadership High School, San Francisco

I CAME INTO THIS COUNTRY from an immigrating family. It was six, seven of us on a street corner, living on a couch. I became a man when I was six years old. That's when I remember making adult decisions, and I felt my childhood just disappear. My goal was to make it and live the next day.

Ever since I was little, I've always lived in my mind. I believe strongly in imagination. What would it be like to reach to the moon? The imagination grew, and now the moon isn't that big of a deal, now it's Mars. Imagination is what makes us desire and reach things, throughout history.

I always wanted to reach out to young people. Capoeira gave me a method to do it. I was 20 or 21, and I was pretty much lost. Then I came in to a class and saw the way the kids were responding to the art, to the movements, to the discipline. Capoeira is a Brazilian martial art, a dance that slaves brought from Africa to Brazil. They used it to pass the time, and people started adding kicks, punches, back flips. It became this amazing martial art. And it just triggered a light in me. I was the oldest in the class, double the average age, and I'm learning along with them.

Now I teach capoeira at the Mission Cultural Center. I have a lot of at-risk kids with low self-esteem. Through the art I can actually help them to have trust and faith in themselves, to find that inner strength that we all have, to prevail against all those forces that try to crush you. I also try to teach them discipline and create a positive network, everybody getting together and working together. I bring a lot of ideas. I'm like a big kid, so I play with them.

Nobody notices how tall they get throughout the year, unless they mark their height on a wall. Wait a year, and you realize you did grow. When you're training capoeira, it's the same way. I see a lot of frustration when people have been with me for about a year. You're getting better and you don't see it. Other people do, but you don't. They don't realize that they are more body-built. I work a lot on that, and on developing relationships and making friends. Being not only honorable and amiable, but the type of person that has weight to their words. You say something, people automatically know you are going to do it.

Right now in the community there are a lot of bad influences. The more you beat people up, the more girls' numbers you get, the cooler you are. The more people you take advantage of, the cooler you are. That's just not good with me. We need the kind of people who actually are cool, and look out for you. That's what I'm working on with my students.

Kids need something to focus them, to bring them back to reality, to get them out of bad influences. They need someone to be there and support them. They want somebody to actually give them the discipline, because that's something they crave. In the Mission, I'm right where I can teach these kids to progress and become an effective community. I'm right where I want to be.

Do Not Let Them Tell You That

Adeola Oredola, interim executive director,
Youth in Action
INTERVIEW BY Josselyn Ramirez
Central High School, Providence

A LOT OF ADULTS JUST TALK AND TALK, and never pay much attention to where young people are, or care what teenagers go through. Youth in Action got started nine years ago by four young people and an adult, who wanted a place where young people had a voice. We wanted to create an organization where everything youth think is taken seriously.

To this day, the students who work with us are part of all of the decision-making we do. They really are committed. They run the organization, they sit on the board, they create programs, they do a lot of the fundraising. They surprise me every day, with the professionalism that they show. Every young person who comes through is impacted by what they do.

We put you through a training process. You choose the programs you are more excited about, and after school you get prepared to teach a workshop, like the nonviolence workshop. You are part of the workshop before teaching it to younger kids, with a team of other people your age. You tell about your personal experiences, and through this work you develop your speaking skills. We put people through different exercises until they get comfortable with their ability to stand before a group. Later, you may speak at a conference, and people will listen. It will be a little scary, but you will do it and you will do well.

I tell young people: Do not let them tell you that you cannot do this. Do not start believing negative things, like "My scores are too low," "I'm not pretty enough," or "I am not good enough." We really try to support every young person, no matter what point in their lives they are in. Sometimes people are in crisis situations and I have felt powerless to help, and worried what would happen. These are the most difficult moments. But even during these moments, people get through, if you stay with them.

Kids coming in may be very shy, not wanting to talk and not comfortable in groups. They may have anger, for whatever reason. Three or four years ago this tall young man comes in, very intimidating. He never smiled in a public setting. He didn't even want to apply for college. We encouraged him to realize the potential he had. Now he is the leader of one of our teams, and one of our best public speakers. He talks to middle school kids about nonviolence. He is just so talented, and he smiles all the time. I just found out

he got into Northeastern, and he is totally excited about going to college.

I believe that young people have the power to do what adults cannot. Four years ago, students raised over half a million dollars to purchase and renovate our four-story building. We work on the first and second floor, and we rent the top floors. So young people here are landlords – they own property and they really do care about the building.

I am young enough to remember what it is like to be your age. I really respect youth. Kids will push me, too, when I do not know if I can do something. I get as much back as I give, or more.

Part of Their Solution

Hector Escalera, probation officer
INTERVIEW BY Yvette Cervantes,
David Maganda, and Jose Mejia
Social Justice High School, Chicago

I GREW UP IN A GANG- AND DRUG-INFESTED community when I was a teenager. I was misguided, and I also had a lot of family problems and legal problems. I was placed in juvenile probation.

One person I had a lot of respect for was my probation officer. She always treated me with a lot of respect, and she was there when I needed the most help. I always looked up to her. So I became a probation officer, and I'm pretty much like her now.

I wanted to come back and help teenagers that had the same problems that I had – to work with them to get away from gangs and drugs, to get educated and succeed in life. A lot of teenagers are in need. Many of them are being misused by adults. They have a lot of issues. And the problems of gangs and drugs aren't going anywhere.

For seven years I've been working in the Little Village community, and it continues to be a very rewarding challenge. I do gang intervention, drug intervention. I advocate for kids in court. I also provide individual counseling about drugs, gangs, school, anything. If a kid can't go to a school because of a gang-related issue, I find another school or get them into a GED program. If a kid has a lot of drug problems, I get them to outpatient or inpatient care.

If kids have problems with their families, I try to talk to them and solve those problems. I understand that families are making a lot of sacrifices financially. Many of them migrated from Mexico to come here to live a better life. But they have problems with their kids. I step in, and I get to be part of their solution. When I help their family, it fulfills their dream. It gets them in the right direction and it makes me feel good. That's the best part of my job.

Once we give kids the help, it's up to them to do the right thing with it. I'm proud to say that a lot of my kids have been able to get their GED. They are in school, they are not abusing drugs, and they are making better decisions. That, for me, is success.

Each One Reach One

Jacquelyn Chaney-Wilson, teacher and volunteer tutor
INTERVIEW BY Alexandria Benton and Jasmine Browne
Mayor's Youth Corps, Tampa

I CAME FROM AN ERA WHERE WE HAD extended family, and I see that is happening less now. You all are a group that no one wants to bother with. There's so many children who just need someone they can talk to. I decided I would be that person, whether it be a mother figure, auntie figure, sister figure. I interact in whatever way teens need me. I get to know them, I hang out with them, see what they are listening to, what they are talking about, what their interests are.

Even when I was a teen, teens came to me, so I would probably have to say that I was born to teach. That was not a route that I was going to when I came out of college. It was a time that blacks could be anything we wanted to. I was going to be one of those people who would make money, but God said no. I taught that year – loved it. I'm a third-generation teacher, and my daughter's a fourth-generation. My grandma taught for 42 years. A lot of my life has been spent in a school, and I have no regrets. I don't know what I would do without it.

It's hard being a parent, it's hard being a teacher, and it's hard being a mentor. Sometimes I need a hug and encouraging words. We need to be encouraged also. And the kids that I mentor, they keep me going. Most of the kids that I used to tutor went to college. One is a lawyer now, one is an engineer. You can be whatever you set your mind out to be, regardless of who you are or where you come from. It's okay to fail, but you don't get stuck there. Sometimes failing brings the best lesson anyone can learn, especially if they want to be successful.

When I grew up, there weren't too many roadblocks for children. We didn't have a lot, but with what we had we were so happy. The family structures that we had, even the extended family… if Miss Sally down the street knew that something was wrong, Miss Sally could whip you. And then somebody would whip you when you got home! We don't have that today – if I beat your child, it's something against your child. Never, ever, ever would I want to be coming up in the time you guys are today. I think you guys are missing out on a lot of love.

Some kids will make it regardless of their circumstance. I just try to plant seeds and hope that someone will come behind me and make them blossom. Some good things are going to come out of some kids, if we all just remember, "Each one reach one."

Saving People from the System

Andrew Williams, music teacher, after-school program
INTERVIEW BY Matthew DelValle,
Stephanie Enright, and Samantha Ortiz
Leadership High School, San Francisco

I HATE WHEN PEOPLE TRY TO BE THE PERSON who gets to define what hip hop is. I grew up on hip hop, but I fell in love with music before I knew what hip hop was. I learned how to play piano before I learned my ABCs. My piano teacher was my babysitter too, and it was like, sit there and have fun. She had a little keyboard and we color-coated the keys. We wrote the alphabet on the stickers, so playing music helped me learn my ABCs, not the other way around.

Wow! I went through a lot of phases. I never thought I was going to be a professional musician. I was thinking more in terms of what was making me happy, and I wanted to keep playing soccer, playing music. I know a lot of people who's rich and unhappy – and a lot of people who are broke and happy. I try to help teenagers figure out what they want to do. I call it "saving people from the system." I like to work with people before there's a lot of pressure to fit in someone's machine.

I like to teach, but you can teach in a lot of different settings. I taught sports and community service in high school; I teach music and recording now. You don't know something unless you know it well enough to teach it. I was sharp when I was in high school. I remember when teachers didn't know what they were doing.

Younger people carry less baggage. They tend to have a positive outlook. There's surprises every day, whether it's about somebody's talent level or just their attitude. The more expectations you have, good or bad, the more you going to be surprised.

One of my first challenges teaching teenagers was just getting over trying to be cool. I'm a younger teacher and sometimes you get caught up in kicking it. You know all the words to the same songs and stuff, but sometimes y'all don't want to listen to me because I look hecka young. That's why I had to grow my goatee out like this, so y'all respect it.

You Do Not Know What You Are Talking About

Willie Stephens, chess teacher
INTERVIEW BY Lysimhour Khiev
Central High School, Providence

GROWING UP IN NEW YORK, I lived in a very dangerous area. I loved extracurricular activities. They gave me an outlet to escape the violence and the dysfunctional behavior around me. I was fortunate to have good mentors. They had experience, stuff I could not get in the normal day of school. They took the time to give me life and love and share their interests.

In junior high school, I remember a summer program where all the best artists, musicians and actors come. An artist, Gregory Phillips, was doing abstract art, and I did not understand or appreciate it. One day I told him he was not doing anything. And he put me in my place. He told me that, even if you do not like abstract art, you need to be respectful and learn from it. He said, "You really do not know what you are talking about, young man.".

He hurt my feelings, but I understood years later that that was the greatest lesson. I graduated from RISD and art was my first love. I looked at books and met famous people, and they gave me dreams to do something positive with my life. This is why I began teaching chess. I am not married and I have no family. Extraordinary circumstances put me into this situation. I could easily get into a higher paying job, but I do this program for personal satisfaction.

I use chess as a vehicle to teach kids another approach to life. The main thing I learn is commitment, indefatigable effort. To be able to take something and follow it to the end. To be able to push yourself to places that you do not think you can find. I am able to push kids beyond their expectations. Whether it be chess, basketball, or creative writing, there is a creative process that kids can become attuned to. And if they can connect with it, they will be successful in what they do.

Most of the time I deal with kids with dysfunctional background. I have developed greater patience. There were a couple of kids who tried my patience and I could have kicked them out. Your ego and pride is involved, but I had to see the greater good. I had to dig deeper, find compassion in my heart, and keep them.

I have been working with teenagers for ten years. I teach in twelve sites; there have been hundreds and hundreds of kids who have gone through my chess pro-

gram. I see them on the streets and around the city. Some have gone to college. My students come back and tell me how they are doing and how they miss the program. Given a dream and an inspiration, they begin to aspire. And once they find success in one area, they transfer this success to other areas. It happens all the time.

Style by the Stylist

Latonya Stevenson, hair stylist
INTERVIEW BY Elise Carroll and Jessica Maggit
ACT Charter School, Chicago

WHEN I WAS A TEENAGER I WAS probably more settled than the average seventeen-year-old. I always read a lot. I had the passion to do hair at a very young age.

After I graduated from high school, I overheard a conversation with some young teenagers. I asked would they mind if I suggested something to them, because I was concerned about the conversation they were having.

I am a hair stylist now. As I'm doing girls' hair, we discuss things that are important to them. I listen to them and try not to judge them. Because no matter how settled I was at their age, no matter how many books I read, I still did things that I know now were not right, especially in my parents' eyes. It's the usual things: I cut classes and went to the game room when I should have been in a math class, so teachers called home.

One young lady called me a few years ago, when she was upset and depressed about a choice she made. As time went by, she couldn't handle the choice she'd made. I talked with her from a spiritual level, never judging her. Later on, she called and said, "I just want to thank you for your words of encouragement and the fact that you never judged me.".

I'm surprised that children today make so many of their choices based on peer pressure, just to fit in. I never had to struggle to fit in, and I never had an issue that I could not talk to my parents about. Today, I tell teens to do things by their own choice. Stand for who you are as an individual.

I try to encourage all the girls to stay in school, further their education. That will help them achieve their goals in life and make things better for their future. I tell them, "No matter what obstacle comes your way, never give up."

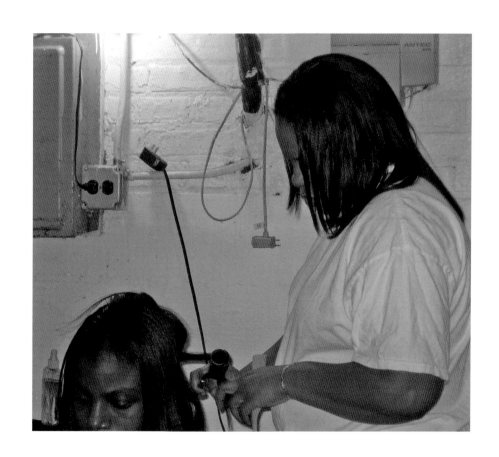

What Makes My Day

Arabinda Banerjee, volunteer mathematics
and Bengali teacher
INTERVIEW BY Shivam Kharod
Mayor's Youth Corps, Tampa

W HEN I WAS A STUDENT LIKE YOU, and I was in India, I hadn't even heard of IT [information technology] or the computer, those were completely new. Engineering did intrigue me, so I went to engineering school and later switched to information technology. Now I work at Citibank in the IT field.

I volunteer at Vidhyalaya, which is a Sunday school kind of organization at the Hindu Temple of Florida. I teach math every Sunday for a couple of hours, and every other week I also teach Bengali language. I like teaching, so I jumped on the opportunity. The teaching here is so much different than the teaching in India, so I try to learn something from the students. It is a mutual learning process.

In the schools here they have a completely different environment than the one where I learned my stuff, so sometimes it is difficult. It's a challenge to have everyone's attention. I understand that sometimes students are not able to pay attention in class, with different distractions and environments. I have to work with that. If I sense that too many distractions are going on, I even let students take a day off or an early-off, because it is too hard to concentrate on something when you have something else on your mind. But anytime a student says, "I get it," I can see the light sparkle in his or her eyes. I enjoy that moment tremendously. That makes my day.

I get the feeling that there is a generational difference in aptitude and skill set. It is so difficult for us adults to do certain things that are so easy for your generation. The difference in the way that learning takes place is a fundamental thing. We were focused on just one thing, but now there is so much bombardment of different kinds of information on every young mind.

The new education should not only teach knowledge as such, but also teach how to quickly make decisions and how to process information quickly. As long as you have the right aptitude, you should be able to compete against the biggest and strongest. But true education is the ability to get what you want without sacrificing certain values. Success in the true sense is not just making money, but doing it the right way, and making good contributions to society and the environment.

Flowers Out of Nowhere

Donna Watson, substance abuse therapist
INTERVIEW BY Docaris Molina
The Met Center, Providence

WHEN I WAS A KID, I liked music and I liked to write. In high school there was some programs where you can learn a little bit about broadcasting, so when it was time for college I decided to go into television. They wanted me to go in front of the camera but I was a chicken. I went into production, behind the scenes.

Three years after college I decided to try cocaine. I tried it once and became immediately addicted. It took me through dark, dark periods in my life. By the ways of God, I broke the chain, and I've been clean for almost sixteen years. You do the math.

My recovery changed my life completely. It helped me get a job in this field, and I've been doing it for almost ten years. I help young people try to do what it takes to get their lives back on track, if they do end up on drugs and alcohol. We do prevention. We go to the high schools and junior highs and talk about drugs and alcohol.

I do anything I can to help young people to not even try it, not even test. If they don't try it, they don't have to worry about it. Nowadays, you are starting to look silly if you do it. It's becoming cool to be a square.

But it's tough out here. Young people have a lot of personal stuff and sometimes they use drugs to escape, which can end up stopping your life and canceling your dreams.

I treat people with dignity, no matter where their choices has put them. They have done some dark things, because addiction makes you change your train of thought. Bad becomes good, in order to get money or get drugs. But as they allow you in, and you are patient enough to meet them where they come in at, they begin to open up and trust, and be willing to learn what it's gonna take.

What makes me happy is to see somebody's life turned around. I see flowers come out of nowhere. People begin to smile. That's my favorite piece of watching change. You can tell when it's real or not.

Beans and Rice for Dinner

Celina Ramos, youth credit union program coordinator
INTERVIEW BY Joshua Pooner
Youth Leadership Institute, San Francisco

I LEARNED EARLY THAT IT'S AN ESSENTIAL thing to save money. My sister and I come from a single-parent household. My mom worked every day in a restaurant, from nine a.m. to eleven p.m. She worked all her life just to provide for us. We lived really tightly; my mom was really careful with her money, but she wasn't able to save for us. We went to live in Salvador for a little while, because of our money situation. But after thinking it through she decided to come back, because she knew that we would be better off in the long run, even if we were eating beans and rice for dinner.

When I was about seventeen, I moved into low-income housing. The community center right next to it wanted youth to participate in creating a new program, and my mother forced me and my sister to go. I was the oldest youth they had, so I became the leader, developing programs for young people – arts, academics, how to apply for college, stuff like that. I got my beginning working with young people there.

Our youth credit union program revolves around economic development. It's important for young people to know how to handle money, because schools don't teach that kind of stuff. It's not a requirement to learn how to balance checkbooks, or how to save money early. Unfortunately, a lot of families are trying to make their dollars stretch to pay rent and buy groceries. It's difficult for them to start saving money, and they don't tell their children to start saving. If we want our young people to become adults that manage their money the right way, it's important that they know how to do it. Just a little saving can help you in the long run. It breaks the cycle of poverty, of thinking that you have to spend the money that you have.

Working here has actually made me improve my own way that I handle my money. If you don't save money, how can you tell other people these things? Now I have to get busy with my own stuff and make sure that it's structured.

I think I always had a good connection with young people. It doesn't just revolve around money. If they have other issues, then we can't work on the important issues that we focus on here. So we need to talk about those other things, too. Sometimes they need help figuring things out – family, gangs, sexuality. All of them are really responsible, and they know that I'm

serious about wanting to help. I'm creating an environment where they can feel free to talk about anything. I would love to keep doing it for a long time to come.

I would like to bring closer the youth, the adults, and the elderly of the community. Parents and elders can create change in the community, by learning new things. When they look at youth and see what their situation is, they stay connected to what's happening.

Success in Small Steps

Iris Holton, journalist
INTERVIEW BY Sheldon Valesco
Mayor's Youth Corps, Tampa

WHEN I WAS YOUR AGE I LOVED TO read. I read everything I could get my hands on, and I wrote poetry and short stories. Now, I'm a staff writer with the Florida Central Bulletin newspaper, and I also write columns on my point of view.

I write articles on both the good and the bad things that happen to teenagers. When kids are going off to college, I interview them and find out what their plans are for their future. I meet a lot of teenagers who are involved in different projects, who receive awards or scholarships. I interact with some who are trying to raise funds for special trips, others that have terminal illnesses. If there's a family in distress, I write articles asking the community to help financially. My primary objective is to find a way that we can help. I have sponsored various organizations, both academic and athletic.

A lot of times you can't talk to people between eight and five Monday through Friday, so to get with the kids I'll do interviews at night and on the weekends. I just rearrange my schedule to accommodate whomever I need to do that for.

Young people now are extremely intelligent, and more outspoken than my generation. I like to hear your points of view, I like to see how you see things. Kids can't wait to leave and go off to college, and I admire that. The idea of leaving home and going away to school – that was frightening to me, but your generation embraced it. It means exposure to other parts of the world. You are not afraid to ask questions. It helps to make you more well-rounded. If you don't ask, you'll never know.

I never saw myself as a mentor. I just do what I do. But people don't see you the way you see yourself. You think I'm a mentor. You can form a bond in a short period of time with someone. When you have to move on, you hope that you made a lasting impression that will help that person as they grow up.

A lot of times, people get depressed when things don't happen overnight. You may think that you're not doing anything, not going anywhere. But as long as you are trying, you are always making progress. Sometimes you measure success in small steps.

Not Angels and Not Devils

Tom Ahn, *director*, college access nonprofit organization
INTERVIEW BY Isidro Fajardo and Einar Sevilla
Leadership High School, San Francisco

I MOVED FROM SOUTH KOREA TO HERE IN 1973. In my elementary school class, everybody was Latino except for one Asian guy (that was me), one white guy, and one black guy. Even my friends would make fun of me, or say racist things. I felt like I couldn't get help, because nobody would understand me. Going to college changed everything for me. I got there and nobody knew me. I could create a new identity for myself.

It's not enough to do something worthwhile – you have to do something that you enjoy. I like thinking about how people learn and the best way to get young people to do what they need to do. I like working in a place where we all work as a team. I like dealing with people, planning, being creative about how to run different programs and raise money. The reasons why some people are rich and some people are poor are not legitimate. It's almost dumb luck. That's almost the worst thing in the world: how wealth gets distributed unequally.

You guys are not angels and you're not devils, you are people who are trying to make the best of what you have. Kids do what they need to do to survive. If you have people living in such poverty, then you are going to have dangerous neighborhoods. Bayfund is so you have the skills and the network and the self-discipline to go to college and build a good life for yourself. So you can help other people, and raise your own family if that's what you want to do, and buy a house, and pay taxes.

Everyone we bring into the program is smart enough. The biggest challenge is to get you guys to have self-discipline and patience and to focus on the long-term goal. If you work hard enough now, you could totally make it. But that's not the easiest thing for everybody. Sometimes I have to bring bad news or get on your case, but I think I set a good example.

Working with kids confirms for me that most of the world has it all wrong in terms of understanding what's valuable and what's not, what's important and what's not. Who has potential, who doesn't – who is worthy of support.

Simple Things

Bob Finer, volunteer basketball coach
INTERVIEW BY Jordan Hiller and Caleb Stenholm
Mayor's Youth Corps, Tampa

I STARTED THIS AS A FRESHMAN IN COLLEGE, as a community service project. I've always been a big basketball player, so I knew I wanted to do something with kids and basketball. I did all the athletics in high school, and played intramurals in college. So I started up a basketball league for twelve-year-olds down at the school. My friend is a gym teacher there, and he was like, "You gotta come play with the boys. They're pretty good, you know, for twelve years old." And he was right.

Kids will tell their friends, and they'll tell their friends. We had twelve or fifteen kids out there a couple Sundays ago, which is like a third of their class. We do it on Sundays between three and five, every other Sunday, pretty consistent for about five years now.

You just end up talking to them and you learn about their lives. Kids are growing up a lot quicker these days, you know. At twelve years old I think they know a lot more now than I did then.

When it started off, it was a class. Now, I don't have to do it, I do it for fun. I enjoy it, I like talking to the kids, we have a good time for a couple of hours. It's just good to keep that sort of relationship within the community.

A few of the kids I started with, I'm actually close to. They are about seventeen now, thinking about college, so it's real easy to give them advice, 'cause I just got out of college. I know what it's like to be in the real world, and I certainly remember what it's like to be in college.

You learn to miss your childhood when you grow older. You get used to this daily routine. You forget the little things that matter to kids. It's good to hear about how simple things can make you happy.

More Than a Job, a Mission

Alexandra Hernandez, prevention program coordinator
INTERVIEW BY Alyssa Piazza and Angelina Romero
Youth Leadership Institute, San Francisco

I CAME TO THE U.S. IN 1984 AFTER A CIVIL war in my country, Nicaragua. I was nine years old. I came from a monolingual Spanish-speaking family, and so in my mind, I had two ways of thinking about things: my own way, and the way my parents thought. Then I had the new way, the "American" way.

I tried to think of things in an analytical way. I remember my friends and me spending a lot of time debating about politics, like the North American Free Trade Agreement that was really gonna have an impact on our trade with Mexico. Proposition 87 came up around that time, when I was in high school. And later Prop 21, the one that criminalized young people as adults for some offenses. I was active in the walkouts against that, in that time. I started doing advocacy in the Mission District, organizing young people around the issues that affected them in their community.

It became for me more than just a job. It became a mission. Being a young Latina woman in the Mission, I felt really passionate about my culture and my heritage, and about the needs of my community. I saw how my community in some ways was disadvantaged and isolated. I wanted my work to be meaningful beyond just the position and the money.

It's important to be grounded in who you are, to take pride in where you come from and what you represent, and then to share that. That's my role in life, to give something back. I came out of this place that's gone through so much. I am a really strong person because of all that growth and experience.

That's why I think adults should work with young people. They make up our community just like children and parents, seniors, and adults. Sometimes certain segments of our community tend to be forgotten. When things like that happen, we see problems arise. When you're young, you need to have a person to look up to. My best moment is when I see a young person I work with overcome their fear of public speaking, or get appointed to a position of decision-making power, or be celebrated in formal or informal ways.

Sometimes when you get older, you get really jaded. But I learned from my youth that you can embrace your dreams and your life in a way that is idealistic and very optimistic. There is a young person in all of us.

Like Drinking Coffee in the Morning

Guillermo Delgado, painter and teaching artist
INTERVIEW BY Nakia Banks
and Annisa Gooden
ACT Charter School, Chicago

I DIDN'T LIKE HIGH SCHOOL. I went to a seminary school for young men who are thinking about becoming a priest. They kicked me out during my sophomore year because they said I had no potential to become a priest. When I was a senior, my girlfriend was pregnant. I was expecting a baby.

I was really bleak, starting to lose hope for the future. I didn't see myself doing anything interesting. I was running out of ideas, approaching a dead end. I thought I would be working at a factory somewhere.

I grew up in a pretty rough neighborhood, on the west side of 26th Street. There's a lot of gang activity there. It was even violent back then. My uncle was my mentor; he showed me how to be streetwise. He taught me to feel confident and how to portray myself so I wouldn't get picked on. How to stay away from all the trouble that was around such as gangs.

I felt like college was part two of high school. With all due respect to Columbia College, I think I picked the wrong school to go to. It's kind of funny, because I work for Columbia now – just at the time it wasn't a good school for me.

I am a professional artist. Fifteen years ago I started teaching by accident. A teacher went to see a show my artwork was in. She asked if I would come in and talk with her fourth-grade class about life as an artist. I was making a living as an artist; I was very successful and good things were happening. I didn't think I was going to be good at teaching.

I discovered I really enjoyed teaching and my students and teachers really loved me. Now I teach and I make art at the same time. I'm surrounded by teenagers. We make art and we talk about art. I end up building relationships with them. A lot of these kids don't have a lot of money or resources. I get to see them go through all the phases. I see them on the road to great things. The way I felt about my teenage years, I don't want anybody to ever go through that.

Every week I dedicate a certain amount of hours to working with young people and teachers. It's a struggle balancing my time. I try not to give up many things. I have to work out, swim, run and bike. If I don't exercise, then I'm not happy. I can't give that up. I have to spend time with my family – they're not happy,

I'm not happy. I like to go out and listen to live music. I still do that, but I can't do it during the week like I used to. I try to stay cool about things.

If I disagree about something some teenager's doing, I try not to react harshly. I think about it and say, Hey, I was a kid once. I try to listen more like my uncle taught me. The people you are mentoring are not always going to live up to your expectations. Think about it as if they are humans and they are going to make mistakes.

Working with you all is like drinking coffee in the morning. Your energy is contagious. I come out here excited, inspired; I want to continue going strong. I never want to go home and sleep.

The Way They Trust Me

José Arnulfo Rodriguez, youth soccer coach
INTERVIEW BY Adriana Canchola,
Alicia Lemus, and José Pimentel
Leadership High School, San Francisco

IN EL SALVADOR IT IS VERY HARD to find a job or even go to college. I worked in a shop cleaning up and learning how to fix typewriters. I would get out of school at eight o'clock in the night and go to my house. I had a lot of bad influences; a lot of youth in my neighborhood were involved in gangs and some also smoked weed and just didn't love life. I proposed to the neighborhood director that we create a soccer team for little kids and another one for teenagers, and this is how I started helping out youth.

It was very hard leaving my country, I had to practically start over and learn new things. But my whole family was here and I was the only one in El Salvador. Now I work as a driver for a company called Cintas. I thank God that I have a stable job in which I can help out my family. And I help out youth here in San Francisco by volunteering after work and on weekends as a soccer coach.

I care a lot about youth and I advise them a lot. It has been a little hard at times to help them out, because I don't speak English. But because of that, I now attend English classes, so I can communicate with those who don't speak Spanish. I tell them that drugs and being in the streets don't get them anywhere, that school is the main thing in their life, that life is hard but it's the way that we all learn and it's what makes us stronger. I tell them to look at certain programs that might interest them. I offer them the idea to join any sports team, instead of wasting their time doing nothing.

My experiences with the youth have been really good. They treat me like their friend and sometimes like a dad. They really listen to me, and many youth don't listen to any adult. They show me their thankfulness by studying, getting good grades, and not getting into trouble. The way they really trust me makes me happy. I'm doing something productive for them, seeing them grow up in a great personality, knowing that in the future they will be amazing persons.

Youth are very important to me because they are the future of tomorrow. If they don't study hard, in the future there would only be poverty. When I was growing up in El Salvador, I learned from my teacher to be original – just simply be who I am. Life is beautiful and we should acknowledge that, day by day.

"Us" and "Them"

Derrick Rollerson, pastor
INTERVIEW BY Jatonne Martin
ACT Charter School, Chicago

WHEN I WENT TO HIGH SCHOOL, I already had an idea in my mind that I wanted to work with young people. I was working with the youth program in my church. We had a boys club and I was helping out with that, and during the summers I served as a camp counselor. A lot of my activities were more focused around the church than school. But I didn't know how you could earn a living doing it.

Now I'm full time in ministry, which I didn't imagine when I was a teenager. I went to school to study insurance. As I was getting ready to graduate, I worked in the career counseling center, helping other students get resumes together and set up interviews. The person in charge said, "Dream and think outside the box. If there is something you want to do and you don't see a position for yourself, create it." That just turned a light on in me. I enjoyed business, but it wasn't exactly what I wanted to do. I wanted to work more closely with people, rather than just shuffling papers around. That opened up a door to go right into ministry, working with high school students.

Working with young people is a passion for me.

We run a high school club on Friday nights. We do a conference in Iowa at the end of the year for the high school students. I am actively involved in camping. I mentor a lot of high school students, trying to help them get prepared for what they want to do in life.

It was a natural progression. I went from being one of the young people to one of the staff helping young people. When I was at camp as a teenager, there was a fellow named Joe Washington. I learned a lot from him, by watching what he did. He wasn't one that would sit down and give you ABC type instruction. He was pretty consistent and firm, and yet he was real gentle and had patience in how he was doing it.

A lot of young guys I work with, they are angry with their dads who are not there. Young people really do need to vent, and I often get a lot of that. I understand it a little bit, but it still hurts. How do I deal with it? I try and overlook the pain and the anger. I still embrace this person as a person that is special to me.

I was mentoring a young man who is now a pastor. I was encouraging him to preach and he was trying to make this transition from being what he called "us" and "them." "Them," he said, was "all you adults."

He explained, "We as teenagers don't necessary want to associate ourselves with adults too soon, because then it makes us have a hard time relating to our peers." He decided to go into ministry full time, and I am really proud of that.

Young people today has gotten burned a lot and they don't trust adults. But I try and tell them, "Don't let anybody stop you from your program." When you get too cynical and angry, it will stop you from doing what you need to do. You have got to have commitment. Learn how to commit yourself to something. Work hard.

Art Teaches People How to Be Better People

Joe Wilson, Jr., actor and teaching artist
INTERVIEW BY Chrissy Stephens
Central High School, Providence

I REALLY WANTED TO BE THE MAYOR OF New Orleans, where I am from. I was going to be a lawyer and be involved in public service. But I got bit by the theatre bug in college, and there was something about being a lawyer or a politician that seemed to limit me.

My folks wanted me to do better than they did. Especially in a community like mine, the art was always a luxury. My parents always said to go to school and be a doctor, a lawyer or a teacher. You will have a family to support, they told me. When I wanted to be involved in the arts, they said: "What! You can make money from that?"

After they put their souls on stage several times a week, most actors want to be alone, to disengage from the community. For me, it is the opposite. I love what I do on stage, I love engaging in that way. But when I get off stage, I want to continue to be engaged in the community, and also feel so passionate about what I do. For the past ten years, something was missing for me – public involvement, to help shape the community, hands on. The part of me that wanted to be a politician was not fulfilled. Coming to a place like Trinity Rep, I knew I had a job. Now I am able to focus on my work and also do some of the things that

I was driven to do before I decided to become an actor.

I love to work in a classroom with young people. I have nothing to hide; my life is an open book. I am here to give you permission to be real with me. When you meet real people, that is contagious. That is the job for a teacher. In a group of kids in a classroom, when one kid opens up, she gives others permission to have courage, to be human, to be authentic. That opens possibilities for you guys – not to cram you into a box. Smart, stupid, Dominican kids here, kids who are poor here, kids who have little bit more money over there.

Art has not always been a luxury. For our ancestors it was the only way to communicate, a way to express ultimate pleasure and pain. Art comes out of the most beautiful and the most awful in life. It is my responsibility to share this knowledge with young people, not using a gun or harmful words. The reason for going into classrooms to work with kids is not to encourage anyone to become an actor. Art is the one profession on the planet whose techniques and tools teach people how to be better people. It teaches you how to listen to the world around you, how to love every aspect of the world around you, how to dream, how to imagine.

Quick Track, Catchy Hook

Simeon Viltz, musician and music production teacher
INTERVIEW BY E'Lisa Davidson
ACT Charter School, Chicago

WHEN I WAS COMING UP, I was basically the same as the youth are now, but with a lot more respect and also a lot more hope. Back then, children respected the elders and also respected their self. We had high hopes that things would get better, instead of thinking of the worst.

Now, I work with kids in music programs throughout Chicago schools. I teach children the fundamentals of music, so that they can use it as a tool of expression. When I started in this nonprofit organization, I noticed right away that the kids treated me different than most instructors. They would feel more free and relaxed around me, which made me feel that they expected more from me. It was a good feeling to be appreciated.

I make the kids that I work with a part of my life. I'm an Underground Chicago artist, and I invite the kids to my shows. I kill two birds at one time: The kids get to spend more time with me, and they also get an insight on the music business. Every child is anxious to make a quick track with a catchy hook, so they can blow up really quick. My job is bringing them down a notch and letting them know how things really work in the industry.

You never know what people are going through, and it is always good to have that figure to look up to, someone you can seek for guidance and reassurance. Some youth feel better expressing themselves to family members; others would prefer if it would be someone outside of the family. We as humans know a lot of things, but we don't necessarily apply them to our everyday life. Nine out of ten children believe everything they see on the television.

The kids are so creative and smart, but they never take the time to notice their own accomplishments. To them, it's nothing. I think it's because they seek to be good in things everybody else is doing. If they have friends that are good at playing ball, then they want to be good at playing ball.

I always want to keep up with the kids I meet. Every child I meet is creative in their own way and I always see the future in their eye. So I want to make sure that they are on track with pursuing their dreams. It makes me feel like a kid all over again, and it keeps me up on my toes. It also prepares me for being a father, since I have a child on the way.

QUICK TRACK, CATCHY HOOK 61

God-Sent Mom

Laura Stringer, foster mother
INTERVIEW BY Charley Pairas
Mayor's Youth Corps, Tampa

I GREW UP TOO FAST. We lived on a plantation, so I just wanted to grow up and get out. I had a sweet mom, but our father left us at a young age. A lot of things that we wanted to do, my mom couldn't afford it. But I always said, "When I grow up, I'm going to be a mom for other kids that their moms can't afford to have things." All through my life, that's what was on my heart. I want to be there for children.

When I heard about foster parents, it would always be something about the kids getting thrown out, the father wasn't taking care of them and the mother was real young. One Friday I just started attending the classes. After about five years, these lil' kids came through and I was lucky enough to get them. Those was my first kids. Oh, Lord, by now there must be hundreds. And it just filled a gap in my life.

It doesn't take much for kids: You have to hug and you have to make them feel safe. They might come to you all disturbed, but once they feel safe, then some mischievous come out, some behavior problems come out. But whenever they feel safe, you got it. My family tell me, "You're not God, you can't change them all." But I can make a difference. It's not about changing them.

Of course they are problem kids! The one thing I did is made their problem my problem. Who do we think we are to pin tags on these kids? We forget that they have a heart, they have feelings. I open my heart, I open my door, and I open my wallet. Unless we reach out, there are not going to be many kids for tomorrow.

If I was able, I would have this big house and just go through the projects, go to the children that need somebody, and pick them up and go shopping for them for school clothes. I would gather them up and take them out to dinner. There are children who have never been out to dinner, have never been to a fair. There are children who don't have a tomorrow if we don't pick them up. Quit pushing them down, and pick them up.

In 35 years we never had a kid get shot up, no guns. I have never seen a stolen car parked in my driveway from none of them. But they had to grow to that. When they walk in, you can't just push them, you got to show some tears every now and then. You got to let them know, "I feel you." If we don't understand them, then they don't care. Teenage boys are just as easy as the babies, once they get your trust. You can't fool

them, you just got to be real with them. You can't bake a pan of cornbread and say that this is a cake.

Many of my kids come now and say, "Oh, mama, how did I take you through that. You so super." I don't need a pat on the back. It might seem that it's putting wear on me, but it's not. My heart feel good, I feel good. When I go into the kitchen to cook, it's a good feeling to know that I have to cook more than one piece of chicken; it's a good feeling to feed all of the kids.

My whole life is different because I had these kids in my life. I'm not helpless anymore. I find something to heal my pain, what I had from a lil' girl. I find joy. I have loved them, I have learned them strength and I've grown from their strength. I'm not even tired, because I know I am a God-sent mom.

Work to Your Limit

Grace Diaz, state senator
INTERVIEW BY Octavio Gomez
Central High School, Providence

NEVER IN THE WHOLE ENTIRE WORLD would I have thought I was going to become a Rhode Island senator. I was like any other teenager: I liked to have fun, find out where the parties were at on the weekends, have a boyfriend and sneak out of my house. I was doing exactly what you guys are doing now! Except we didn't have the technology you guys have.

My mother raised four children by herself. And later, becoming a single parent of five children myself, I had to face so many challenges. When you take care of children, they depend on everything you do – education, support, putting food on the table, molding them with character to become later a good citizen. Sometimes I have to put my own goals aside because I have to place my kids' needs and goals first. But eventually that frustration becomes energy that makes me reach my goal and my dreams.

When I was doing my 2006 campaign, teenagers in the neighborhood were a very important piece of the process of getting me elected. They were door-knocking, making phone calls and working on Election Day, and so many other things. Most of the teenagers I have around me are not even eighteen years old, and I see in them the skills, the desire, the attitude to be leaders and eventually replace me.

Young people teach me a lot, their initiative and how they are open-minded and hungry to learn. You don't know until you sit with them, you talk to them, and you see what they want. Because they were asking me questions but were telling me also what they wanted. They need to have somebody leading them in some directions, and I want to take the action.

The earlier that teenagers can learn about politics, the better citizens they can be in the future. Right now, I try to be the bridge. Any kids who approach me and want to be an intern, want to be working in the State House or to know more about politics, I open my office for them. I'm planning different activities for the summer, getting the teenagers busy so that they don't have any opportunities for thinking of doing wrong things. I want them to have opportunities for jobs. I want to pay the teenagers so that they could partici-pate in cleaning the neighborhood, learn about politics, and also get some money for their personal expenses.

The human being has to work to your limit of strength and effort to reach what you want. I don't believe in things that are mild. You have to go to one side – either you are, or you are not. The teen age is very fragile, and there's a lot of temptation. I want to see young people really understand the difference between choosing the right and the wrong thing. Sometimes, just a second can change a life.

How This Book Took Shape

Kathleen Cushman, What Kids Can Do

STUDENTS CARRIED OUT THIS PROJECT during the course of a semester, under the guidance of adults who allocated ten to fifteen sessions to the work. Some took it on as a class or advisory group project, others in an after-school enrichment program. Only a small selection of the resulting products appear in this book; all told, over 200 students participated in four cities.

The project required as its tools only digital cameras and simple tape recorders; What Kids Can Do provided a modest number of those, which students shared among themselves. With that – and with energy and commitment – any group could take on a similar project, capped by a publication of its own design.

The skills of interviewing, transcribing, editing, and photography require expert coaching, however, and for this, we offer here an array of teaching guides created for this project. Organizing the project also takes some doing, so we also provide help in identifying and contacting mentors, as well as a consent form giving permission to publish their words, if desired.

In truth, the most difficult part of this process is also the most important: helping young people recognize the adults who care about them, outside of their homes and classrooms. Many young people believe they do not know such people, and this only deepens the gulf between generations that badly need each other's help. When we began this project, we addressed this painful issue directly. And, as we spoke together about the ordinary people whose actions and attitudes matter to them, their faces began to lighten. What about the proprietor of the corner store, who gave them good advice and sometimes paying work? What about the youth choir director at church? Thinking about their everyday lives, students kept asking whether people like that count as "mentors that matter."

They certainly do. As our teacher reflections reveal, everybody benefits when adults and youth begin noticing each other in positive ways, whether that happens one by one or in a public ceremony. We hope that you will freely use our materials, creating local versions of Mentors That Matter in communities far and wide.

Teacher Reflections on the Mentors Project

On student learning outcomes

This was an unusual "assignment for students." It required that they make a decision regarding a person outside of school who makes a difference in this world, interview and photograph the person (using a tape recorder to record the conversation), then transcribe and write a story from the person's point of view.

They are used to writing essays or first-person accounts, but most of our students are not experienced in telling a story using someone else's words. They were intrigued by the "journalistic style" of reporting. Once they got it, understood it, and had the copy to play with, they really liked telling the story.

The photography became a really fun addition to the project. Again, they are not accustomed to using photography to tell stories. Most loved doing it.

Bianca Gray and Richard Gurspan
Central High School, Providence

For many of the students at the Met, the project was an incredible experience. I will share one story that I believe illustrates the power of the Mentors That Matter journey. One young man particularly struggled through the majority of the project, completing work at the last possible moment, refusing to communicate with his mentor, and exhibiting anti-social behavior in the group. Up until the day of the celebration, he maintained that he would not be attending the event. When I alerted him that I had spoken with his mentor he agreed to go, dragging his feet the entire way to City Hall.

And then something amazing happened. At the event I watched as this same young man stood before the crowd and proudly introduced his mentor and spoke about his mentor's role in his life. This young man was confident and thoughtful as he spoke. His mentor expressed his gratitude to his mentee and shared his pride in watching him grow from a child into a man. After receiving their awards, the two hugged and took their places in the audience. I watched as they huddled closely, grinned ear to ear, and looked at each other's awards, oblivious to the goings-on around them.

After the event I spoke with the student and told him I was very proud of his efforts. He replied, "I'm proud of myself too." For many of the Met students the journey from picking a mentor to the final show was a long and difficult one, with many requirements and challenges. It was also a journey that offered them opportunities to develop critical skills, confidence in themselves, and, perhaps most important, deeper relationships with important adults in their lives.

Cary Donaldson, The Met Center, Providence

My students really valued the project. One student said, "That's when our class came together." It was an opportunity to connect with a mentor in a different way. It was a way to make the relationship more formal and more public. In addition, students got to participate in a project for an actual book, so they found a great real-world sense of writing and revising. The students who had the chance to work with an accomplished editor were lucky. Too often, only their teacher looks deeply at their academic work.

Mark Isero, Leadership High School, San Francisco

I am not sure all of my students "got it" until the event, when they saw all the people and the very impressive posters of their work. They also learned project development, transcribing, how to read the transcription critically to pick out the most interesting parts, and then how to fit those parts together. They had to meet deadlines and complete a rather extensive project in a relatively short time. They sometimes worked in pairs, and in some cases they experienced the frustration of not having their partner respond in a timely fashion.

I hope they also learned what it means to adults to have a meaningful role in the lives of young people. It would be nice if this project motivated them to "pass it forward."

Rebecca Heimstead, Mayor's Youth Corps, Tampa

My students found gratification in the writing process, especially those whose feelings about writing have been that writing is a struggle, that it's hard work, and that it's never finished. Seeing their work professionally published, and knowing that it would be, inspired and excited them. One IEP student reflected that this project and process made her feel empowered to make choices about her writing, about what she thought was good.

Meg Arbeiter, ACT Charter School, Chicago

On what mentors gained

They felt honored to be selected by *kids.* They seemed surprised at how well prepared the students were for the interview; some students were really skillful in how they listened and asked questions based on the mentor's responses.

The feedback we got was extremely positive, mentors thanking us for letting them be a part of the project. They told us it made a difference, that the connection they made was meaningful. Some of the students and new mentors actually made new friends, someone to admire or to aspire to be like.

Bianca Gray and Richard Gurspan
Central High School, Providence

At the celebration, it was clear that the mentors appreciated the response. After getting their medal and certificate, they walked to the middle of the stage and gave their thanks. One mentor remarked that this was the first time in 30 years that he had been recognized. Another said it was nice to be honored for doing something he loves.

Mark Isero, Leadership High School, San Francisco

I spent time with mentors at interviews, photo sessions, and the final celebration. The mentors my students selected had vastly different careers and stories. Yet across the board the mentors were honored and excited to be asked to share their experiences and deepen their connections with young people in their lives. A few mentors who did not work with young people in their day-to-day lives especially impressed me. They seemed to appreciate the honor of being acknowledged by youth on a whole other level. I watched as they brimmed with pride at the celebration. How cool.

Cary Donaldson, The Met Center, Providence

Most often adults are presented awards by other adults, so this project, which had them being recognized by young people, was far different. Monsignor Higgins, when he received his medal and plaque, said it was perhaps the most significant award he had ever received, since young people selected him – and Monsignor has received many, many awards.

Many of these adults are just "regular people." The public recognition – at the event, and later via the display at Old City Hall, the article in the *Tampa Tribune,* and the ongoing exhibit at the Children's Board – gave them far more exposure then they would have ever received otherwise. I don't believe there was a single mentor recognized who does what they do for the recognition, but it is very nice when people publicly acknowledge the contribution they have made.

Rebecca Heimstead, Mayor's Youth Corps, Tampa

In both formal written and informal verbal feedback, the adults have expressed their appreciation for being interviewed and honored as mentors. For many, this was the first opportunity they had to be publicly recognized and appreciated for the good work that they do. One of the mentors told me later that she had the final piece on the wall in her home. All of them thanked me at the exhibit.

Meg Arbeiter, ACT Charter School, Chicago

On what teachers learned

I was a bit nervous about all the steps that required kids to be out in the community, use technology, listen, photograph and come back with good material to use for the telling of the story. Some needed an adult to be simply present as they navigated about, or a few worked in twos for moral and technical support.

Most of the kids really surprised us with what they

brought back. A few were shy and did not have enough copy; we asked them to reconnect, and they did and brought back better material. Most brought back too much, but the material was useful and focused on the project's theme. It was great to see them be so eager to connect, excited about these new connections (for some), and caring about the outcome a great deal!

Some really want to be published and they worked with that in mind. It was great to see them challenging themselves.

It took more than we expected – more time, more attention for each student – but we saw the majority of students very engaged and interested. They loved the extra photos, and wanted copies. They were really engaged, thoughtful, well organized, great company, and fun. It turned out to be a great project.

Bianca Gray and Richard Gurspan
Central High School, Providence

I realized that my curriculum needs an overhaul. The past few years, my curriculum has become less authentic and more complicated while I have steered toward more rigor. There was simplicity in this project that I can use next year as I refine my curriculum. The students knew exactly what they had to do, and it was rigorous, and the deadlines were real, and they were accountable to an outside evaluator. All the assessment people would say it's a perfect project.

Mark Isero, Leadership High School, San Francisco

While this project certainly had its challenges, overall I found it to be an incredibly rewarding project. Having developed and facilitated photography and writing workshops for young people before (on my own), I found the various handouts and instructional tools very helpful. At the same time, taking part in the project afforded me the space to learn about my new city and the amazing people who care about its young people. Incredible!

Cary Donaldson, The Met Center, Providence

It was such a rewarding project for me that I would like to be able to do it again. I can't believe I am saying that, because it was very time consuming to pull off, especially since the students were new to Youth Corps and not yet adept at communicating via email, meeting deadlines, etc. The process of identifying the mentors was interesting; it was rewarding to see that the teens had people who were not parents or teachers who had made a significant positive impact on them. It was also nice to be able to recognize fellow adults who support young people. The students looked very grown up at the event; they spoke well and did an outstanding job. Seeing the faces of the mentors at the celebration made every minute of work more than worthwhile.

Rebecca Heimstead, Mayor's Youth Corps, Tampa

While it has been a priority for me for my entire teaching career, this was the first time I created an opportunity for my kids to write for an authentic audience and publish their work. That is *huge*, and the impact on the students' learning, pride, and gratification in their writing is obvious. I will constantly seek more ways to publish their work outside of school.

Also, the interview and transcribing process is one that I am now integrating into my teaching of writing as well as studying. It's brilliant – why didn't I do this before?.

Meg Arbeiter, ACT Charter School, Chicago

Unintended or serendipitous outcomes

The project underlined the need to connect with the community in a meaningful way as opposed to having speakers come, speak, have a short Q&A, and go on their way with barely a memory left. Kids really remember their interviews, details about what happened, where they were, what they said. They were correcting us on details all the time, to make sure that we, the teachers, got it right. And a few made new important connections to wonderful people in the community. We saw real sparks and followup and unscheduled visits and new interest. One student and one teacher even received a mention in a theatre program, a thank you for contributing to the play the mentor was working on at the time. The student was *very* happy; she felt deeply appreciated and noticed.

Bianca Gray and Richard Gurspan
Central High School, Providence

I didn't intend to change my curriculum so much. One great outcome is that the achievement gap was not as prevalent. There wasn't predictability. More struggling students did well on this project than on others I've assigned. Because an outside evaluator (without bias) made decisions about which narratives were top quality, it made me think about ways I could look at student work in a different way. Finally, what was great is that quality came not just from what work they did but which person they chose. The choice of mentor was as important as the hours of interviewing, transcribing, and editing.

Mark Isero, Leadership High School, San Francisco

I think it pulled my new students closer together. It also allowed me to see them speak publicly, which I normally do not have much of a chance to do before the end of their year with me.

The extended display at the Children's Board may have additional outcomes. At the celebration, the school superintendent also mentioned something about displaying the posters at another location. I will follow up with that one.

I also think there will be outcomes that we never know about. People may read the narratives and call a former teacher to say thank you, they may reach out to that neighbor child who always plays alone, and perhaps they will volunteer to coach a youth sports team.

I hope my students who were lucky enough to

participate and nominate and interview a mentor will understand the importance of adults in the lives of young people and elect to be a mentor someday.

Rebecca Heimstead, Mayor's Youth Corps, Tampa

For my students, the greatest outcome was seeing themselves as real writers. That is something I have always strived for, but this succeeded on such a greater level. It extended into the powerful writing that they did as they wrote memoirs of transformation, which beautifully paralleled their own transformation into writers. One student, a brilliant and talented young man, discovered this year, at last, that he is a writer and wants to pursue it as well as filmmaking, and that is why he chose Columbia College, which he will be attending in the fall. This is a student who a year ear-lier was going to drop out of school and get his GED. And there is so much more evidence of this, as students wrote in their reflections on the final project.

Personally, it provided a rare opportunity for others, including my mom, to see the work that I do and the brilliant young adults that I have the privilege to work with.

Meg Arbeiter, ACT Charter School, Chicago

Books and Resources

Forty-Cent Tip: Stories of New York City Immigrant Workers, by the students of three New York public international high schools, edited by What Kids Can Do (Next Generation Press, 2006).

India in a Time of Globalization: Photo Essays by Indian Youth, a project of Adobe Youth Voices and What Kids Can Do, edited by Barbara Cervone (Next Generation Press, 2008).

In Our Village: Kambi ya Simba Through the Eyes of Its Youth, by the students of Awet Secondary School in Tanzania, East Africa and What Kids Can Do, edited by Barbara Cervone (Next Generation Press, 2006).

Shout Out: A Kids' Guide to Recording Stories, by Katie Davis, downloadable from Transom.org, a project of Atlantic Public Media; contact info@transom.org.

Nominating a Mentor That Matters

GUIDELINES FOR STUDENTS

Look outside your immediate family.
We hope to honor mentors that reach out to people other than those who are related to them. So we suggest that you only nominate a family member if that person also connects in a significant way to other teenagers.

Look outside your school.
We want to honor mentors whose job may not require them to work with youth, but who reach out to teenagers anyway. Please nominate a teacher or coach only if that person goes above and beyond the expectations of their job, reaching out to youth in other ways.

Look for people who share their interests with young people.
Artists, musicians, filmmakers, and writers may be on your list of people who matter to teenagers in your community. Look too for people who connect through sports or outdoor adventures, through church, or through volunteer activities.

Look for people who introduce teenagers to the world of work.
You may know someone who takes on one or more young people as interns in the workplace, helping them learn things they would not otherwise know. Hospital workers, tradespeople, or professionals all might be on your list. Whether or not the job is paid, these adults can open important doors to teenagers.

Look for people who help kids who are having trouble.
You might know someone who keeps an eye out for young people who are struggling – either in their schoolwork or in their personal lives. In a group or one by one, adults like this often step in just in time to turn a teenager's life around.

If you have trouble thinking of someone

Get suggestions from outside your group.
Take the nomination form to homerooms or advisory groups, and collect ideas. It's not necessary for you to personally know the adult you interview – if you are convinced that some local youth are positively affected

by contact with the adult, that's enough for a nomination. (Examples: Someone else's choir director; someone's driving school instructor, someone who teaches a babysitting course at the local hospital.)

Do some research about what organizations connect with youth in your community.
Does your city have a Big Brother or Big Sister initiative? A youth theater group or arts center? A popular slam poetry venue? A youth hockey team? A suicide prevention hotline? If so, somebody is behind it, and that person probably matters to kids. (You can go visit such places, and find out from the kids who are there.)

Team up with one or two other students to visit one adult.
The interview might actually go better if more than one student is involved. Afterward, your transcribing might also be easier with one student typing and the other doing playback. And it might be easier to get a good photo if one person can be taking pictures while the other talks with the adult.

NOMINATION CHECKLIST

- What is the name of the mentor adult you hope to interview?

- How can you can contact this adult to ask for an interview?

- What does this adult do that brings him or her in contact with teenagers in your community?

- In what place(s) does this adult carry out the activities you describe?

- About how often does this adult connect with teenagers in this way? (Every day? Every week? Every month?)

- Can you estimate how many teenagers this adult connects with in this way? (You could be the only one, or there could be other individual teenagers, or a group.)

- Are these activities part of this adult's job, or does the person do them informally?

- In your own words, please say how this adult makes a difference in your own life or in the lives of other teenagers you know.

Interviewing a Mentor That Matters

GUIDELINES FOR STUDENTS

INFORMATION

Name of adult to be interviewed: _____

Phone number of adult to be interviewed: _____

Address where the interview will be held: _____

Date and time when interview will take place: _____ at _____ o'clock

Student interviewer(s) and photographer(s):

Name: _____ Phone # _____

Name: _____ Phone # _____

Who will conduct the interview? _____

Who will take the photograph? _____

REMINDERS

☐ Show up on time at the place you agreed to meet.

☐ Start by asking the interview subject to fill out and sign the release form (see page •••).

☐ Turn on the tape recorder and make sure that it is working.

☐ Record the interview from start to finish.

☐ Take the photograph of the person you are interviewing.

☐ Label the tape cassette with the name of the interview subject and the date.

☐ Return the release form, the camera, and the tape recorder & cassette to the group.

INTERVIEW QUESTIONS

A good interview comes from asking questions that do not invite yes or no answers!

To prepare for an interview with a mentor, think about your own experiences with a mentor. For example:

- Describe a time when a mentor really helped you.

- Tell of a time when an adult really believed in you.

- Talk about a time when someone pushed you to do something you didn't think you could do.

Now think about how to connect what you experienced with what your subject experienced in the role of mentor. Some possible questions:

- What were you like when you were my age?

- What do you do now? When you were my age, would you have imagined that?

- Can you tell me more about the interactions you have with teenagers?
  - What do you do with them?
  - How many young people are involved (either now or in the past)?

- When did you start making this kind of connection with youth?
  - How did it happen, and why?

- How do you make time for this kind of connection in your life? What kinds of things do you give up in order to make time for it?

- When you were around my age, did you spend time with any adults that mattered to you?
  - What was that like for you?
  - What did you learn from those interactions that still matters to you now?

- Are there things you've learned in your life that you feel are important to pass on to my generation? (Work skills, knowledge, ideas, values, things that have happened in your times . . .)

- Tell me about your "best moment" as a mentor – a time when you felt like you were really helping someone.

- Tell me about a time when you encountered an obstacle while mentoring someone.
  - What got in the way?
  - What did you do about it?

- Tell me about a time when you really learned something about mentoring.

- Tell me about a time when you really learned something from someone you were mentoring.

- Does anything surprise you about the young people you spend time with now?

- What are some interesting things you've noticed about my generation?

- Do you ever stay in touch with the young people you've connected with, after they move on?

- Can you say anything more about what is satisfying for you about the time you spend with people my age?

*Use the space below to write down any other questions
you might ask the person you will interview.*

_____

_____

_____

_____

_____

_____

_____

_____

_____

_____

_____

MENTOR RELEASE FORM

*If you plan to publish the interview in print or on the
Internet, you will need written permission from the person
whose name, words, and image you use. Ask the intervie-
wee to sign a general release like the model that follows:*

I agree to be interviewed and photographed in connection with a student project (the "Work"), sponsored by
_____ . I hereby grant the right
and permission to display and publish my name,
photograph, likeness, and statements and comments,
in whole or in part, without prior review, in all formats
of the Work. I warrant that the accounts told, written,
or furnished by me are original with me and do not
violate any copyright, personal, or proprietary right.

I have read the foregoing and fully understand its
contents.

_____

SIGNATURE   DATE

_____

PRINT NAME AND ADDRESS

_____

Turning Interviews into First-Person Essays

GUIDELINES FOR STUDENTS

Abe Louise Young, What Kids Can Do

Interviews are a wonderful tool for documenting history and social or cultural issues, and also a great way to learn about people's lives. These tips will help you turn a spoken interview into a clear piece of writing that will hold the interest of an outside reader.

As your first step, you will transcribe the interview, writing out everything the person said, exactly as they said it.

Once you have that transcript, you are ready to begin editing it into a first-person essay in the voice of the speaker. You become a kind of "co-author" with the person you interviewed. The words are theirs, but you choose what parts to use and in what order to arrange them. You present their story to a reader. This is an honor and a challenge.

Before you start

Before you begin editing the interview, know the length of the final essay you will produce from it. A good length is 500 words, or about two double-spaced pages.

If you are doing this work on the computer, be sure to save two files: the "unedited transcript" and the transcript that you are editing into an essay. You will need to go back often to check the original words.

Editing your interview transcript into a completed essay takes time, and it should go in several stages.

Deciding on your focus

Because it is a conversation, every interview has many more words than you will use in the final essay. When looking at a long transcript, many people find it hard to choose the important parts.

For this reason, it helps to know your goal. Do you want your essay to focus on a certain theme, like "work" or "childrearing" or "war"? Or do you want to create a portrait of the person as a whole? Once you make this decision, you can begin to determine what to save and what to cut. Ask yourself:

- What is unique about this person?

- How does this person see the world?

- What does this person know that others do not?

- What details reveal this person's time period, place, or community?

- What specific personal details does this person share?

Think about what you really want the reader to know about your narrator. By getting this clear, you can present a strong picture of who the narrator is.

What's important to keep?

Start with the printed transcript of the complete interview. Read it several times. As you read, use a highlighter to mark statements that you might want to include.

- Mark the passages where you can best feel the speaker's energy – joy, sadness, worry, fear, anything that brings the person to life on the page.

- Look for moments of description and observation. When you can hear, see, smell, touch, or taste what the narrator is talking about, that's a good sign that it should go in the essay.

- Look for statements of meaning – passages where the narrator tells why something matters to him or her. These will also help your reader care, so they can make your essay stronger.

What you should cut

Much of what people say in an interview is not "essay material." For example,

- Take out "filler words" like "um," "ah," and "you know."

- Take out unimportant comments. (Ask yourself, "Does this give readers something they need to know in order to 'get' this person?")

Sometimes, a speaker will talk about the same subject – food, for example – in different parts of an interview. First, group these passages together. If they say the same thing in different words, keep only the part you like better.

When in doubt, cut it out!

Organizing the narrative

Interviews let people remember and make sense of their experience out loud. For this reason, your narrator may talk in roundabout ways, and touch on many different topics.

As you edit the interview transcript, look for a balance between creating organization and keeping a natural flow in the narrator's speech.

You may move the pieces of the interview around to find an order that makes sense to the person reading. But you also want your reader to experience the narrator's thought patterns. The order in which someone shares feelings can show something interesting about how the person sees the world.

Look for a strong beginning – something that makes you want to keep reading, to find out more. A student interviewing a car-wash owner started the narrative like this:

Not again! It's raining for the third time this week; I'll have to take the day off. The water steals my job; my tips vanish in the air. Everyone who owns a car goes out on rainy days so the water can do its work for free. They do not see that I need to wash their car to survive.

Look for an ending that leaves the reader with something to think about. For example, in the car-wash essay:

How I miss the sunny days in the Dominican Republic. That is the place I would rather be, instead of here at the car wash, where I keep on praying, "Please, God, don't cry today, let me work the whole day."

Staying true to the speaker's voice

Everyone talks in a style that belongs to that person. Your readers will want to "hear" the natural voice of the narrator.

Do not change the speaker's words in order to make them "better" or "more descriptive" or "good grammar." If your narrator speaks in slang or a dialect, don't change their words to standard English.

However, you may leave out unnecessary words, to make a passage shorter or more clear. You can indicate where you cut words by typing three dots (. . .), which is called an ellipsis. For example, in this interview with a survivor of Hurricane Katrina:

This is a place that is unlike any place in the world. There's dancing everyday in the street . . . . Right now, if I just take this cane and derby I got, and I start singing a beat, people will follow me and just go down the street. You can't do that nowhere else. I will never leave New Orleans. I will die here.

You may also need to insert words, to make clear the speaker's meaning. Put brackets around any words you have added. For example, in the previous example, you could do this:

This [the New Orleans French Quarter] is a place that is unlike any place in the world.

When the speaker uses several languages

You may interview someone who speaks several languages – and that is an important part of who they are. Statements made in a native language might have the most impact if you present them in that language.

In that case, write the foreign language in italics. Then, translate for the reader. Put the translated words in brackets.

In the example below, Paul Phillips, Jr., describes his father, a self-trained veterinarian and descendant of slaves. His father could communicate in both German and English. Paul describes an interaction in both languages:

A husband of the household, unknowingly to his wife, called my father for a tooth extraction of their pet dog. The dog screamed, causing the lady to come to the door. Upon finding out what was going on, she said, "Ich murdu auch den Schwartzen dasz thun wasg weisg." ["I don't think this black man knows what he's doing."] *Not looking up from his work and to the surprise of both, my father calmly replied, "Ich weisg."* ["I do."] *That lady was really surprised!*

Explaining the context

You may need to add a note before or after the essay, so that the reader understands things that the speaker has not directly addressed.

For example, a brief introduction or end note could explain the relationship between the speaker and the person who conducted the interview. Or it could tell why and where the interview took place. For example, sentences like this could go in italics before or after the essay:

Sari Alborni interviewed her mother Carmela Alborni about emigrating to America in 2006. They spoke in their home in San Francisco.

Reading the essay aloud

When you have made your interview text into a shorter narrative essay, print it out and read it aloud (either to yourself or to another person). As you do, you will notice places that do not sound natural, or places where you can cut unnecessary words. Your ear will tell you things that your eye will not catch.

After you make the changes, read the piece aloud again. Keep repeating the process until you have an essay that captures both these key elements:

- The focus you wanted
- The essence of the person who is speaking.

Checking your piece with the interviewee

Once you have the essay finished, show it to the person who was interviewed. Make sure that your work has not somehow changed the meaning or tone of what that person intended to say. Together, you can make the final changes, so the essay stays true to the speaker, and at the same time is short and clear enough to engage the reader.

Don't forget to make a clean printed copy of the final piece to give to the interview subject. Together, you will have created something of great value – both for the speaker and for all the readers your essay will reach.

How to Take Good Photographs

GUIDELINES FOR STUDENTS

Barbara Cervone, What Kids Can Do

How do you begin to take good photos? The first thing to remember is this: The photographer, not the camera, takes great photos. Second, remember that you master photography by doing it – experimenting and learning by trial and error.

The following tips should get you started. Some will have more meaning after you've gone out, shot a bunch of pictures, and analyzed the results.

Camera basics

Learn about the moving parts.

Find and practice operating your camera's shutter, zoom, and LCD monitor/display screen. Learn what each of the mode settings on the dial next to the shutter is best used for. Learn how to review pictures you've taken, and how to erase a picture. Get to know the items in the menu and the icons that come up on the display screen, and learn how to turn specific features on and off, or change them.

Hold the camera steady.

A basic rule of photography is to hold the camera steady. If the camera moves while you are taking a picture, the result will be a blurry image. The only thing that should move when taking a picture is your finger on the shutter. The more you can steady your arms, the sharper your pictures will be. When holding the camera, also be sure that you don't have a finger in front of the lens or the flash.

Hold the camera level.

Another basic rule of photography is to hold the camera level. Otherwise, your pictures will come out sloping to one side or another – cock-eyed. Look for the horizontal lines in the scene you are photographing (like the horizon!) and use them as guides.

Know how to set your camera's automatic focus.

A third basic rule of photography is to get the focus right, so that the image is sharp. Rely on your camera's automatic focus. When you press the shutter button halfway down, the camera adjusts the focus automatically. Remember to press the shutter only halfway – and then press the shutter down fully. If you press halfway down, then let the shutter come back up and then press down fully, you will lose the focus you set.

Learn to control the flash.

All digital cameras have an automatic flash, but that doesn't mean you should always use it. When taking photos outdoors, it is sometimes good to turn on the flash to illuminate the subject, especially if he or she is in the shade. (If your camera is set on automatic flash, it normally won't go off outdoors.) At times, you may be taking a picture indoors and it would be good to turn off the flash – when your camera will typically trigger the flash. Using the flash indoors can result in unnatural skin color and harsh glare in your photos.

Understand the zoom lens.

It is tempting to over-use your camera's zoom lens. It lets you get close to a subject without feeling like you are putting the camera in the person's face. It can also help to create a focal point in a large landscape or to take pictures of people naturally going about their routine without their knowing you are photographing them.

But there is a trade-off. The more you zoom into a subject, the more the resulting image is affected by "camera shake." And when the camera shakes, photos come out blurred.

If you are taking photos in the daytime or in other highly-lit situations, you don't have to worry as much. The more available light, the quicker the camera's shutter opens and closes, and the less chance that camera shake can affect the result. However, if you are taking pictures of moving subjects or in low-light situations, you must be careful to keep the camera very steady.

Unfortunately, your digital camera's "picture preview" mode, with its lack of detail, may not show that the photographs you took were blurred. You may only find out after you copy the pictures to your computer.

Have enough memory capacity.

It's terrible to be in the middle of taking pictures and then run out of memory space. Always have enough memory capacity in your digital camera. Here are general guidelines:

- 3 megapixel camera – get at least a 128MB card
- 4 megapixel camera – get at least a 256MB card
- 5 megapixel camera and above – get at least a 512MB or 1GB card

Set your camera for high resolution and low compression.

One of the most important reasons for packing a big memory card is so that you can shoot at your camera's highest resolution and lowest compression, both of which take up memory space. Why? Because these two factors – resolution and compression – hugely affect how your photos will look when printed or blown up on a computer screen. A photo taken at a low resolution – 640 x 480 ppi (pixels per inch) – will look fuzzy when enlarged beyond 4 by 6 inches. Compression works the other way. If compression is set too high, image quality goes down.

All digital cameras allow you to set resolution and compression levels. (At the end of this tip sheet, there is a technical section that defines these terms in more detail.) It sounds complicated, but here are suggested settings (for some of the newest cameras).

USE OF IMAGES	RESOLUTION	COMPRESSION
Internet, email	640 x 480	Standard high compression
4" x 6" print	1632 x 1224	Standard high compression
5" x 7" print	2048 x 1536	Fine low compression
8" x 10" print or larger	2816 x 2112	Fine low compression

Your camera's megapixel capacity also makes a difference. The more megapixels, the higher you can set the resolution. It's good to work with a camera that has at least 3 megapixels. Again, use the biggest memory card you can get, so that you can fit lots of high resolution/low compression photos (which take up more megabytes) and avoid the frustration of running out memory just when you are about to snap the perfect picture!

Shoot more

With digital cameras, there is no added cost to taking more photographs. Shoot more, not less. When creating a photo essay, it's hard to know which pictures, in the end, will best help you tell your story. So snap whatever catches your fancy. When you take multiple shots of the same scene, you increase the likelihood that one of the pictures will be a winner.

Turn off your camera's "date function."

Photos that appear with the date in the corner are unusable when creating a professional-looking slideshow or exhibit.

Photo composition

Move in close.

It's always good to move in closer to your subject. Almost any scene will benefit from your taking several steps forward. The goal is to fill the picture area with the subject you are photographing. That way, you can reveal telling details, like the expression on a face.

As tempting as it is to use your camera's digital zoom to get close to your subject, the image quality is much better when you use the "sneaker" technique – walking up to your subject. As noted earlier, "zooming" can result in blurry images, especially when the light conditions are low or the subject is moving. The best choice may be a compromise: Get as physically close to your subject as you can, then use the zoom lens a bit (but not all the way) to inch in closer.

Your camera's "macro mode" can also help you close in on small, still objects; make sure you allow the camera to focus properly before depressing the shutter button fully. You do this by pushing down the shutter half way, waiting a second for the camera to focus, and then pushing down the rest of the way – without taking your finger off the shutter.

Although it's hard to get too close, it can happen. The closest focusing distance for most cameras is about three feet, or about one step away from your subject. If you get closer, your pictures will be blurry.

Anticipate the moment.

With digital cameras, there's a delay of several seconds from when you press the shutter button and when it takes the picture. If you are shooting anything active, make sure you press the shutter button down long before your subject is at the position you're trying to capture. You may need to take many pictures to make up for the delay factor.

Look your subject in the eye.

When taking a picture of someone, hold the camera at the person's eye level to unleash the power of a gaze or smile. For children, that means stooping to their level. Your subject need not always stare at the camera. All by itself, the eye-level angle will create a personal feeling that pulls you into the picture.

Take some vertical pictures.

Do you want to take pictures of tall statues, buildings, trees, or other tall structures, yet you can't seem to get the whole subject in the picture? Turn your camera 90 degrees to the side (vertical), then focus on your subject and snap the image. Suddenly those tall items that couldn't fit in the digital camera's viewfinder before may fit perfectly. And don't stop with turning your digital camera 90 degrees. Experiment with other orientations.

Trust your instincts.

In the end, trust your own instincts when it comes to composing your photos. As you frame the shot, move the camera and explore the scene. When you find an angle or composition that feels good to you, take the picture immediately. Then get several more shots.

Analyze your work.

Look at the pictures you have taken and ask some questions. Did the image turn out as you planned? Do you like the composition? Could you have closed in more on the subject? Would the picture have come out better if you had turned the camera vertically?

Lighting

Always take lighting into consideration.

Next to the subject, the most important part of every picture is the lighting. It affects the appearance of everything you photograph. On an older face, for example, bright sunlight from the side will emphasize the wrinkles, while the soft light of a cloudy day will soften them. Don't like the light on your subject? Then move yourself, or your subject.

Rely on available light as much as possible.

Learn how to turn off your camera's automatic flash – and then turn it off. Turn to the flash only when:

(1) you are shooting in bright conditions and simply need a tiny bit of "fill" flash

(2) the lighting is poor and you have no alternative but to rely on your on-camera flash.

If you are not sure whether the picture requires the flash, experiment. Take a shot without the flash and look at it on the LCD monitor/display screen. Then take one with the flash. See which looks better.

Avoid red-eye.

When taking pictures with your digital camera, do your subjects look like they have red eyes? This is common when taking pictures with the flash on. If you notice this problem, first check if your digital camera has a feature called "flash – remove red eye" (most do) and make sure it's on. If yours doesn't have such a feature, don't fret. Most image editing programs (like Photoshop) have a "remove red-eye" feature.

Use the "presets" in difficult lighting.

Many digital cameras come with what are called "preset modes" that help you take good pictures in difficult lighting conditions. Here are some modes found in popular digital cameras. (Read your digital camera manual for details on which presets your camera supports.)

- Night: Just what it says; takes better pictures in low-light conditions.

- Portrait: Brings clarity and attention to the subject while making the rest of the picture slightly blurred.

- Landscape: Sharpens the entire picture, instead of just the focus area.

- Sunrise/Sunset: Adjusts the camera's settings for these trickier light situations.?

- Motion: Adjusts the camera's exposure time settings to allow for quicker shots of moving subjects, such as people in sporting events.

Know the range of your flash.

If you do use the flash, make sure you aren't taking the picture beyond the flash's range. Pictures taken beyond the maximum flash range will be too dark. For many cameras, the maximum flash range is less than fifteen feet – about five steps away. What is your camera's flash range? Look it up in your camera manual. Can't find it? Then don't take a chance. Position yourself so subjects are no farther than ten feet away.

Turn around to avoid the sun.

When taking outdoor photos, position subjects so that the sun is behind you. If the sun is directly in your field of view, your subjects may look overexposed and washed out. With the sun behind you, enough light reaches the subject to show a wide variety of color without washing out features like skin tones.

Don't shoot subjects or objects in front of a window. If you are taking a picture indoors and the subject is close to a window, the person or object may turn out too dark. The camera's automatic light meter will lock onto the light coming in from the window, leaving your subject under-exposed and mostly black – the opposite of the washed-out white look of over-exposed pictures.

Some definitions

What is a memory card?

Often referred to as digital film, a memory card is the recording device where digital image data is electronically stored. Memory card types include Compact-Flash, Memory Stick, Secure Digital, SmartMedia and xD-Picture Card. Memory cards come in various capacities, from 16 megabytes to several gigabytes. The larger the storage capacity, the more images a memory card holds.

Handle a card carefully, according to the manufacturer's instructions. Insert it into the camera or memory card reader in the correct direction and never forcefully. Turn off your camera before inserting or removing a card, but never shut it off or remove a card if a photo is being written (saved) to the card.

What is "image format"?

This is the manner in which digital images are stored. There are numerous ways to store an image, and the most popular are jpeg (pronounced "jay-peg"), gif, tiff, and bitmap. By looking at the end of the file name after the period, you can identify the format. For example, picture.jpg is a jpeg file. Jpeg (Joint Photographic Experts Group) is the most common format; it's how digital cameras normally store the pictures they take.

What are pixels?

Pixels are the building blocks of digital images. Every digital picture is made up of thousands of pixels (or dots). The number of pixels in each image affects the quality of the picture resolution. Cameras are rated by their megapixels (meaning one million pixels). These days, all cameras have at least three megapixels, some as many as ten. The number of pixels is important when in comes to printing a picture: It determines how sharp the picture will look when printed at different sizes. The more pixels, the bigger you can print a picture without it's looking grainy or distorted. Most new cameras today come with four to seven megapixels.

What is "resolution"?

Resolution is tied to pixels and, again, defines the sharpness of your digital image. Resolution is often defined as how many pixels per inch (ppi) your image has in both its height and width – though it relates to the size your image appears on the computer monitor and not the actual physical dimensions an image prints. Still, as noted above, the more pixels in an image, the bigger it will print without losing quality. Digital cameras allow you to change image resolution. For example, sizes on a four megapixel digital cameras can be, from highest to lowest: 2272 x 1704, 1600 x 200, 1024 x 768, and 640 x 480 pixels.

Mentors and Youth Participants

This list names all mentors honored by student participants in the Mentors That Matter project. Mentors' names are followed by the names and affiliations of the students who interviewed them. An asterisk marks the ones included in this book; to see all the photographs and narratives, visit the website www.whatkidscando.org.

CHICAGO, ILLINOIS

*Tom Bailey, television producer
by Bridgett Rivers, ACT Charter School

Marisela Bazan, dance instructor
by Yvette Cervantes, David Maganda, and Jose Mejia, Social Justice High School

Patricia Buenrostro, graduate student, community activist
by Oscar Almanza, Linda Mijangos, and Andrea Ramirez, Social Justice High School

*Guillermo Delgado, painter, teaching artist
by Nakia Banks and Annisa Gooden, ACT Charter School

Kimeco Dodd, musician and editor
by Bianca Exson and Trinece Mosley, ACT Charter School

James Duke, video producer, college student
by Randall Watkins, ACT Charter School

*Georgia Dunbar, school bus driver
by Kendra Clark and Brittney Williams, ACT Charter School

Sherri Edmonds, JROTC instructor
by Jaleesa Edmonds and Stephanie Jones, ACT Charter School

*Hector Escalera, probation officer
by Yvette Cervantes, David Maganda, and Jose Mejia, Social Justice High School

Samuel Garcia, violence prevention worker, community activist
by Ivan Chavez, Reynaldo Dominguez, and Rut Rodriguez, Social Justice High School

Jason Godinez, Boys and Girls Club leader
by Adriana Alvarez, Maribel Cuenca, and Fanny Garcia, Social Justice High School

Rico Gutstein, college professor, school design team member
by Richard Barraza, Norma Emeterio, and Neftali Negron, Social Justice High School

TaWanda Johnson, church youth leader
by LaWanda Douglas, Jaleesa Thomas, and Shamika Wysinger, ACT Charter School

Eric Morris, basketball coach
by William Dunbar and McKinley Florence,
ACT Charter School

*Derrick Rollerson, pastor
by Jatonne Martin, ACT Charter School

Amy Rudd, volunteer tutor and adviser
by Kasheika Cobbins and Schererazade Edwards,
ACT Charter School

*Dwayne Sanders, student government adviser
by Shakira Robinson, Christopher Smith, and Vivian Taylor,
ACT Charter School

Ava Kadishson Schieber, writer and Holocaust survivor
by Sehara Garmon, Kyle Harris, and Steven Newson,
ACT Charter School

Tina Scott, abuse counselor
by Litkeshia Coffee, ACT Charter School

*Latonya Stevenson, hair stylist
by Elise Carroll and Jessica Maggit, ACT Charter School

David Stovall, college professor, volunteer tutor
by Jazmin Johnson, Erika Owens, Rogelio Rivera, Viviana
Ruiz, Karla Sarmiento, and Rocio Villavicencio, Social
Justice High School

*Simeon Viltz, musician and music production teacher
by E'Lisa Davidson, ACT Charter School

Lolita Voss, dance instructor
by LaDawn Voss and Kiya Wiggins, ACT Charter School

Shai Afsai, English teacher, DelSesto High School
by Ruby Olivares and Bryan Burgos, Central High School

Joseph S. Almeida, state representative
by Jonathan Gartomah and Octavio Gomes, Central
High School

Noreen Bamford, sixth grade teacher
by Marlene Corcino, Met Center

Bill Beatini, Boys and Girls Club director
by Harold Threats, Met Center

*Steve Bianchini, restaurant chef
by Cheyla Luciano and Janaye Ramos, Met Center

*Len Cabral, storyteller
by Marcus Page and Jason Page, Central High School

Angela Coburn, dance teacher
by Evelyn Robertson, Central High School

Cesar Cuevas, actor, street food vender
by Randy Herrera and Rafael Gutierrez, Central High School

Tyler Denmead, executive director, Project Urban Arts
by Linette DeJesus, Central High School

*Grace Diaz, state senator
by Octavio Gomez, Central High School

Elizabeth Elencruz, youth activist, Rhode Island College
by Lubi Lora and Jennifer Portuhondo, Central High School

Trixy Ferrell, street worker, Institute for the Study
and Practice of Nonviolence
by Stevona Small, Met Center

Teny O. Gross, executive director, Institute for the Study and Practice of Nonviolence
(*twice*) *by Freddy Gonzalez (Met Center) and by Marry Chum (Central High School)*

*Natasha Johnson, double-dutch coach
by Stephanie Carew, Met Center

Dorothy Jungels, artistic director, Everett Dance Theatre, Carriage House Players
by Valerie Poirier, Central High School

Patrick Lynch, state attorney general
by Nathan Bessell, Central High School

Harold Metts, state senator and school vice-principal
by Angel Liriano, Central High School

Simon Moore, director, college access program
by Abel Hernandez and Randy Herrera

*Adeola Oredola, interim director, Youth in Action
by Josselyn Ramirez, Central High School

Ricardo Pitts-Wiley, artistic director, Mixed Magic Theatre
by Rudy Cabrera, Central High School

Peter Rios, high school football coach
by Thomas Pina, Met Center

Sokeo Ros, dancer, Everett Dance Theatre and director, Case Closed
by Mariela Ramirez and Yesenia Paulino, Central High School

Sebastian Ruth and Minna Choi, director and musician, Community MusicWorks
by Jolene Nunez and Patricia Genao, Central High School

Megan Sandberg-Zakian, associate director, Black Repertory Company
by Marilis Hopp, Central High School

J. Lynn Singleton, president, Providence Performing Arts Center
by Miguel Pimentel, Central High School

Raymond Smith, community outreach ministry
by Precious Monteiro, Central High School

*Willie Stephens, chess teacher
by Lysimhour Khiev, Central High School

*Donna Watson, substance abuse therapist
by Docaris Molina, Met Center

Marilyn Wentworth, seventh grade teacher
by Paris Watson, Met Center

*Joe Wilson, Jr., actor and teaching artist, Trinity Repertory Company
by Chrissy Stephens, Central High School

Chantel Wyllie, adviser, the Met
by Franni Diaz, Met Center

SAN FRANCISCO, CALIFORNIA

*Tom Ahn, director, college access nonprofit organization
by Isidro Fajardo and Einar Sevilla, Leadership High School

Teresa Almaguer, coordinator, youth leadership program
by James Li and Alessandra Ortiz, Leadership High School

Ines Barbosa, youth adviser, college access organization
by Bertha Medina, Leadership High School

Danny Chao, youth worker, YMCA
by Luisa Sicairos, Youth Leadership Institute

*Andres Fernandez, capoeira teacher
by Edwin Lara, Leadership High School

Ben Flores, pastor
by Mauricio Ponce de Leon, Leadership High School

Allan Frank Frias, dance instructor
by Lody Faddoul and Alex Barksdale, Youth Leadership Institute

Irene Garcia, dancer and teacher, Bolivian dance group
by Priscilla Fallas and Laura Rubio, Leadership High School

*Alexandra Hernandez, prevention program coordinator
by Alyssa Piazza and Angelina Romero, Youth Leadership Institute

*Edith Lewis, police officer
by Brittanny Tucker, Leadership High School

Jim McGarry, teacher, activist
by Catherine Everett and Claire Swarthout, Youth Leadership Institute

José Ochoa, volunteer athletic coach
by Fernando Miguel Ramirez and Edwin Siliezar, Leadership High School

*Celina Ramos, youth credit union program coordinator
by Joshua Pooner, Youth Leadership Institute

*José Arnulfo Rodriguez, youth soccer coach
by Adriana Canchola, Alicia Lemus, and José Pimentel, Leadership High School

Jason Standiford, youth adviser, college access organization
by Brian Barragan, Miguel Martinez, and Bradley Perez, Leadership High School

Michael Vigil, youth minister and counselor
by Rene Ontiveros, Leadership High School

*Andrew Williams, music teacher, after-school program
by Matthew DelValle, Stephanie Enright, and Samantha Ortiz, Leadership High School

*Naomi Wright, assistant, after-school program
by Prisca Cheng, Leadership High School

Neilsen Zulueta, volunteer tutor
by Richard Lopez and Nathaniel Zulueta, Leadership High School

TAMPA, FLORIDA

Leland Baldwin, lawyer, church youth director
by Liz Jennewein and Austin Lambert, Mayor's Youth Corps

*Arabinda Banerjee, volunteer mathematics and Bengali teacher
by Shivam Kharod, Mayor's Youth Corps

*Jacquelyn Chaney-Wilson, teacher and volunteer tutor
by Alexandria Benton and Jasmine Browne, Mayor's Youth Corps

Eileen Charette, founder, Project Outreach; Key Club adviser
by Gabriel Gari and Nena Garga, Mayor's Youth Corps

Kenneth Christie, school volunteer
by Khobi Smith and Austin Queen, Mayor's Youth Corps

*Bob Finer, volunteer basketball coach
by Jordan Hiller and Caleb Stenholm, Mayor's Youth Corps

*James Geiger, counselor, Anytown program
by Simon and Manuela Muñoz-Alvarez and Alexa Holcomb, Mayor's Youth Corps

Susan Gray, student intervention specialist
by Solange La Puente, Mayor's Youth Corps

Cynthia Gries, director, girls music revue
by Sara Diehr and Allison Walsh, Mayor's Youth Corps

Shawn Harland, volunteer basketball coach
by Shawnna Harland and Kelsey Schweiberger, Mayor's Youth Corps

Brenda Hiers, teacher, tutor and youth group leader
by Christina Warner, Mayor's Youth Corps

Monsignor Laurence Higgins, pastor, parish school
founder *by Katarina Herce and C.J. Hernandez, Mayor's Youth Corps*

*Iris Holton, journalist
by Sheldon Valesco, Mayor's Youth Corps

*Brother Damian McCullagh, elder at Tampa Catholic,
copy machine guru
by Ryan Carter and Taylor Neal, Mayors Youth Corps

*Doctors Susheela and Ravindra Nathan, pediatrician
and cardiologist
by Shreya Narayanan and Alena Ransom, Mayor's Youth Corps

Monica L. Sierra, circuit court judge
by Gabrielle Gonzalez, Mayor's Youth Corps

*Laura Stringer, foster mother
by Charley Pairas, Mayor's Youth Corps

Lorrie Sullebarger, Girl Scout leader
by Amber Sierra and Kari Holbrook, Mayor's Youth Corps

Marilyn Wannamaker, Junior Women's Club adviser
by Christian Nunez, Mayor's Youth Corps

Acknowledgments

TEACHERS AND MENTORS

Meg Arbeiter
Academy for Communications and Technology (ACT)
    Charter School, Chicago

Cary Donaldson
The Met Center, Providence

Bhumika Gor
Social Justice High School, Little Village
Lawndale Campus, Chicago

Bianca Gray
Central High School, Providence

Richard Gurspan
Central High School, Providence

Rebecca Heimstead
Mayor's Youth Corps, Tampa

Mark Isero
Leadership High School, San Francisco

Michele Paolella
Youth Leadership Institute, San Francisco

Tracy Van Duinen
Social Justice High School, Little Village
Lawndale Campus, Chicago

SPECIAL THANKS

MetLife Foundation

Small Schools Workshop, Chicago

San Francisco Public Library Teen Center

San Francisco Center for Essential Small Schools

Seewan Eng

Will Okun

CREDITS

Kathleen Cushman
WKCD project coach

Barbara Cervone
Photography editor

Abe Louise Young
Contributing editor

Sandra Delany
Book design